The development of th

1750–1914

New Studies in Economic and Social History

Edited for the Economic History Society by
Michael Sanderson
University of East Anglia, Norwich

This series, specially commissioned by the Economic History Society, provides a guide to the current interpretations of the key themes of economic and social history in which advances have recently been made or in which there has been significant debate.

In recent times economic and social history has been one of the most flourishing areas of historical study. This has mirrored the increasing relevance of the economic and social sciences both in a student's choice of career and in forming a society at large more aware of the importance of these issues in their everyday lives. Moreover specialist interests in business, agricultural and welfare history, for example, have themselves burgeoned and there has been an increased interest in the economic development of the wider world. Stimulating as these scholarly developments have been for the specialist, the rapid advance of the subject and the quantity of new publications make it difficult for the reader to gain an overview of particular topics, let alone the whole field.

New Studies in Economic and Social History is intended for students and their teachers. It is designed to introduce them to fresh topics and to enable them to keep abreast of recent writing and debates. All the books in the series are written by a recognised authority in the subject, and the arguments and issues are set out in a critical but unpartisan fashion. The aim of the series is to survey the current state of scholarship, rather than to provide a set of prepackaged conclusions.

The series has been edited since its inception in 1968 by Professors M. W. Flinn, T. C. Smout and L. A. Clarkson, and is currently edited by Dr Michael Sanderson. From 1968 it was published by Macmillan as *Studies in Economic History*, and after 1974 as *Studies in Economic and Social History*. From 1995 *New Studies in Economic and Social History* is being published on behalf of the Economic History Society by Cambridge University Press. This new series includes some of the titles previously published by Macmillan as well as new titles, and reflects the ongoing development throughout the world of this rich seam of history.

For a full list of titles in print, please see the end of the book.

The development of the French economy, 1750–1914

Prepared for the Economic History Society by

Colin Heywood
University of Nottingham

CAMBRIDGE
UNIVERSITY PRESS

Published by the Press Syndicate of the University of Cambridge
The Pitt Building, Trumpington Street, Cambridge CB2 1RP
40 West 20th Street, New York, NY 10011-4211, USA
10 Stamford Road, Oakleigh, Melbourne 3166, Australia

The Development of the French Economy, 1750–1914 first published
by The Macmillan Press Limited 1992
First Cambridge University Press edition 1995

Printed in Great Britain at the University Press, Cambridge

A catalogue record for this book is available from the British Library

Library of Congress cataloguing in publication data

Heywood, Colin.
The development of the French economy, 1750–1914 / prepared for the Economic History Society by Colin Heywood.
p. cm. – (New studies in economic and social history)
Includes index.
ISBN 0 521 55276 1. – ISBN 0 521 55777 1 (pbk.)
1. France–Economic conditions. I. Economic History Society.
II. Title. III. Series.
HC275.H38 1995 95–18678
330.944–dc20 CIP

ISBN 0 521 55276 1 hardback
ISBN 0 521 55777 1 paperback

CE

Contents

Tables and maps

Tables

Map

Note on references

References in the text in round brackets relate to the numbered notes at the end of the text. References within square brackets relate to the numbered items in the Bibliography; where page numbers are given, they are printed in italics, for example [76, *231*].

Acknowledgements

I should like to thank Serge Chassagne, Olena Heywood, Patrick O'Brien and Roger Price for comments on early drafts of this work. I should also like to make the customary reference to my feelings of indebtedness to the numerous historians, above all those based in France, whose publications I have drawn from but whose contribution cannot be recorded in a short pamphlet.

1
Introduction: the outlines of a debate

In 1789, France electrified the world with her revolutionary ideals, providing inspiration for generations of political radicals. During the 1800s, it was French military prowess that came to the fore, as the Napoleonic armies shattered the foundations of a whole series of régimes in continental Europe. And at the end of the nineteenth century, Paris could claim to be the cultural capital of the world: a Mecca for writers, composers and painters. But what of the French contribution to material progress? Was France as impressive in the creation of wealth as she was in these other fields? At first sight, somewhat paradoxically, it would appear not. Among contemporary observers, notably those from aristocratic circles who had tasted the delights of Paris and the Côte d'Azur, French people had the reputation of living above all for pleasure and frivolity. The English, by contrast, were known more for their 'industriousness and plodding patience' [23, *13*; 66, I, *14–63*]. Anyone interested in learning about the new industrial civilization emerging during the eighteenth and nineteenth centuries was therefore likely to go to England, or, later on, to the United States and Germany. Celebrated French exports, such as fine wines, perfumes and silks, also gave the impression of a country that was more agricultural than industrial, more attuned to an *ancien régime* of luxury and elegance than to the machine age [30, *470*]. The historical literature in its turn recites an all too familiar litany of failures and mistakes that held back French economic development: the handing over of land to inefficient peasant farmers; the reluctance to exploit potentially important inventions; the hesitation in expanding beyond the limits imposed by the family firm; the preference for overseas instead of home investments; the timorous sheltering behind tariff barriers; and so on and so forth. In the economic sphere at least, France can easily be depicted as one of the 'also rans', lagging behind her neighbours in a number of performance indicators [25; 58; 104, *112–204*].

And yet, over the last decade or so, historians in France as well as in the 'anglo-saxon' world have produced a stream of books and articles enthusiastically proclaiming the need for a radical revision in French economic history. During the 1950s, Rondo Cameron described the French performance as 'disappointing', but in 1983 he stood on his head and asserted that 'in fact, the French economy performed very well in comparison with other industrializing nations' [17; 19, *4*]. Out went the themes of 'stagnation', 'backwardness' and 'retardation'. Out too went the stress on sources of weakness in the economy. Instead came the suggestion that the French had been remarkably successful in carving out their own path to development. It followed that the dynamic forces at work in the economy were worth highlighting, as well as the inevitable obstacles to growth. The ugly duckling had suddenly become a beautiful swan [29; 97; 91; 14].

In this work, we are bound to ponder the extent to which such a violent swing in the pendulum has furthered our understanding of the topic. Revisionists would see themselves using new sources and new perspectives to extend the scope of the debate beyond the old orthodoxies of the 1940s and 1950s. In particular, they can point to the limited data on national incomes available to early commentators, and to the danger of judging French economic development by the extent to which it conformed to the British 'paradigm'. But they are surely open to the criticism of being carried away in their enthusiasm for a radical alternative, risking an unduly favourable assessment of the French performance [26; 59]. The undertow from the older interpretation remains strong. Indeed, the most recent econometric analysis of the French economy during the nineteenth century concludes that change was slower than statistics assembled in the 1960s would suggest. Its reworking of the figures emphasizes 'the permanence of traditional structures, the high level of agricultural income until the early 1880s and the obstacles in front of industrialization' [73, *270*]. To pursue the analysis, this study will focus on two broad questions. First, what were the main characteristics of French economic development? And secondly, which of the various possible explanations for the French performance are most convincing? Answers to the former necessarily rely heavily on quantitative types of evidence, leading to diverse assessments of the French performance. Discussion of the latter has traditionally lined up historians emphasizing *material* influences (such hoary old chestnuts as coal shortages or slow demographic increase) against those preferring to stress *social* and *cultural* factors, notably the deficiencies of French entrepreneurs. If this general framework for the debate has been established for some time now, its content has been enriched over the last few years by a late flowering of French economic history. Beside the long tradition in France of writing regional histories, there has emerged an interest in producing scholarly monographs on individual firms, industries, and groups of businessmen. Social historians too have begun to explore topics of interest for our purposes, such as the formation of industrial dynasties among the bourgeoisie or management strategies for controlling labour. Our aim here will be to give some hint of the wealth of material available, and some insight into the complex issues it has raised.

2
The performance of the French economy

Most historians like to open their discussion of the French economy with a flourish of statistics. Their desire to measure the performance of the economy is entirely laudable. But a word of warning: eighteenth and nineteenth century statistical sources are notoriously unreliable! Mayors in rural communes, for example, had a reputation for compiling official statistics with a scant regard for accuracy. It is hardly surprising that historians have occasionally arrived at widely divergent appreciations of particular economic variables, notably the growth of agricultural production in the eighteenth century, or levels of industrial productivity in the nineteenth. This should not be taken as a counsel of despair. One of the great strengths of many recent studies has been the application of economic theory to historical data from France. Quantitative historians have displayed considerable ingenuity in overcoming the drawbacks to their sources, using tithe registers, for example, to estimate agricultural production, or information on raw materials to calculate the output of an industry. They have also agreed international standards for drawing up national accounts, which permit some confidence in comparisons made between France and her major rivals. Nonetheless, students of the subject would be well advised to grit their teeth and look closely at the 'sources and methods' sections of the various studies, in order to familiarize themselves with the nature of the exercises involved. They should also be aware that for all the precision arrived at by historians, historical statistics cannot aspire to the accuracy expected of their late twentieth century counterparts.

Having grasped the nettle and decided to use statistical evidence as a foundation, one might hope that the growing volume of data

Table 2.1 *Annual rate of growth of gross national product and population, 1860–1910* (benchmark years are three-year annual averages)

	Total GNP (a)	Population (a)	GNP Per capita
Austria-Hungary	(1.76)	0.78	(0.98)
Belgium	2.04	0.91	1.12
Denmark	2.94	1.06	1.86
France	1.41	0.16	1.25
Germany	2.57	1.17	1.39
Italy	1.05	0.66	0.39
Netherlands	2.05	1.15	0.89
Russia	2.25	1.27	0.96
Spain	(0.61)	0.48	(0.13)
Sweden	2.70	0.73	1.96
Switzerland	2.08	0.81	1.25
UK	1.87	0.89	0.97
Europe	1.88	0.92	0.96

Source: Bairoch, 'Europe's Gross National Product: 1800–1975', *Journal of European Economic History*, 5 (1976): 283.
(a) Total annual increase including effects of territorial changes.
Note: The degree of rounding off of the figures does not imply a correspondingly low margin of error.

available would point to some kind of consensus on French economic development. But this has not proved to be the case. Protagonists in the debate have disagreed on the significance of various performance indicators, as they seek to buttress their case for a generally negative or positive assessment. Take the obvious starting point: long-run figures on economic growth. The usual approach, which we will follow here, has been to judge the performance of the French economy by comparing it with those of other developing nations.

Table 2.1 reproduces estimates of growth rates for France and some of her neighbours between 1860 and 1910, plus an aggregate figure for Europe based on 19 countries. They are for the gross national product (GNP) at market prices. Figures in brackets have a particularly high margin of error. Before attempting any comparisons, we should note the relative lack of homogeneity in the various estimates of growth rates. Paul Bairoch draws attention to a lack of uniformity in the methods used to reconstruct GNP data and divergences in international price structures. For these reasons a considerable margin of error must be taken into account. We have therefore taken the relatively late period 1860 to 1910 as our starting point, since the data become more reliable at this stage. It is immediately apparent that if the growth of *total* GNP is considered, then France performed relatively poorly. Her growth rate of 1.41 per cent a year was well below the European average of 1.88 per cent, and indeed she appears to have been outstripped by all her rivals, with odd exceptions such as Italy and Spain. On this basis, the French economy in the nineteenth century might well be described as 'retarded'. However, Table 2.1 also documents the fact that France had the slowest growing population in Europe: an increase of a mere 0.16 per cent a year at this period. It follows that her economic performance was more impressive when measured in *per capita* terms. The growth rate of French GNP *per capita* between 1860 and 1910 was 1.25 per cent: sufficient to lift her above the European average of 0.96 per cent, and to place her among the front runners.

A similar pattern can be discerned when earlier periods are considered, though admittedly on the basis of more limited evidence. In Table 2.2, Maddison shows France once again performing unimpressively in the growth rate of her total output between 1820 and 1870, but emerging closer to major competitors such as the United Kingdom and Germany in the growth rate of GDP per head of population. For the eighteenth century, we are obliged to fall back on comparisons between France, Britain and the Netherlands, given the absence of data for other countries. Even with the troubled years of the Revolutionary and Napoleonic Wars included, Table 2.2 suggests that growth in output per head of population was remarkably close on the two sides of the Channel during this early period. Which then is the best performance indicator? Should one concentrate on the growth of total output, and dismiss the more favourable *per capita* results as a statistical illusion, attributable to a slow demographic increase during the nineteenth century? Or should one agree with François Crouzet that product *per capita* is 'the genuine criterion of

Table 2.2 *Growth of output (GDP at constant prices), 1700–1870 (annual average compound growth rate)*

	Total GDP		GDP per head of population	
	1700–1820	1820–1870	1700–1820	1820–1870
Austria		(1.4)		0.7
Belgium		2.7		1.9
Denmark		1.9		0.9
France	0.6(a)	1.4	0.3(a)	1.0
Germany		2.0		1.1
Netherlands	0.1	2.4	−0.1	1.5
Sweden		(1.6)		0.6
Switzerland		(2.5)		1.7
United Kingdom	1.1	2.4	0.4	1.5

Source: Maddison, *Phases of Capitalist Development*, pp. 44–5.
(a) 1701/10–1820

economic progress' [29, *170*]? The latter view would be more acceptable to most economists and economic historians, and so it will be proposed here as the best single measure of economic welfare available. It is certainly the starting point for most of the recent revisionist writing in French economic history.

However, before any overall assessment of French economic growth can be made, two additional points must be considered. First, the levels as well as the growth rates of *per capita* incomes in Europe can be measured. The results show France in an intermediate position, rather than an obvious leader or laggard. According to the estimates of both Bairoch and Crafts, France ranked seventh in 1910: behind Great Britain, Belgium, Denmark, Switzerland, Germany and the Netherlands, but ahead of Austria, Sweden and Italy [4, *286*; 26, *51*]. Second, the peculiar rhythms of French economic growth have attracted the attention of historians. For many years there was a tendency to denigrate the French performance since there was no obvious 'great spurt' to match the British Industrial Revolution or the rapid growth of the German economy in the late nineteenth century. This line of argument is now discredited [76]. Recent research has emphasized that in general economic growth in nineteenth-century Europe was slow by contemporary standards, and that in the particular case of France, a gradual, 'unobtrusive' path to development had its own merits [91]. Yet one cannot ignore the fact that France experienced 'a growth which was without exceptional acceleration but punctuated by phases of marked slackening in pace' [1, *13*]. The upheavals of Revolutionary politics and prolonged warfare during the 1790s and 1800s brought the first such period of deceleration. According to an oft-quoted phrase from Maurice Lévy-Leboyer, this was a 'national catastrophe', which destroyed the efforts of a generation and permitted the British to take a decisive lead over their old rival [67, *29*; 30, *295–317*]. The 'Great Depression' years of the late nineteenth century brought the second run of lean years. Lévy-Leboyer and Bourguignon have pointed to the extended pause in economic growth between 1860 and 1886 as unique to the French experience. The long-term consequences were, once again, pernicious, the suggestion being that France fell behind her main competitors during an important period of liberalized trade and technical innovation [73, *1–13*]. Not surprisingly, then, a note of caution has been sounded in certain evaluations of French economic growth. Crouzet summed it up as 'not brilliant, but quite creditable' [29, *170*]; Crafts as 'respectable but certainly not outstanding' [26, *67*]. Such conclusions would appear to strike the appropriate balance between the extremes of gloom and exaltation to be found in the literature.

Further dissension among historians comes to the surface when we move from the essentially *quantitative* changes associated with economic growth (defined as a sustained increase in *per capita* incomes) to the *qualitative* changes implied by the term economic development. Critics of the French performance have often focused on the lack of structural change in the economy before 1914. More specifically, they have asserted that the French economy placed too much emphasis on farming, failed to take full advantage of large-scale production and never overcame marked regional disparities [25; 58]. The implication is that more rapid structural change would have stimulated an increase in average incomes. Hence we may have here the first hint of an explanation for the rate of economic growth in France. But the problem with this line of argument, according to the revisionists, is that it assumes the British path to development to have been the optimum. In other words, the performances of other countries are judged either explicitly or implicitly by the extent to which they conform to the British model, with its rapid run-down of the agricultural sector and its relatively early shift to an urban-industrial type of economy. The alternative proposed by the revisionists is to suggest that there are various possible paths to development, appropriate to the circumstances of the countries concerned, and none should be treated as a paradigm.

Take first the alleged overcommitment to agriculture. The evidence here appears incontrovertible. In 1910 France still had 41 per cent of her labour force employed in agriculture and extractive industry, compared to 15.1 per cent in Britain. Yet the contention that *per capita* output in France would have increased more rapidly had resources been redeployed from agriculture to industry on the scale observable in Britain between 1780 and 1914 is open to question. O'Brien and Keyder accept that, historically, the long-run increase in *per capita* incomes realized by the developed economies has been associated with the relative decline of the agricultural sector. But they cast doubts on 'the idea that structural transformation is an exogenous variable in the growth process, capable of rational manipulation'. They and others are surely convincing in their assertion that French industry could not have absorbed the huge quantities of labour that running down agriculture on British lines would have required. The primary sector in France was simply too big for such a transformation to be envisaged. Indeed, what is now clear is how unusual the British performance was among the nations of nineteenth-century Europe. Crafts shows that France was consistently close to the 'European Norm' for the share of labour employed in agriculture and mining at a given level of income, while Britain was 'something of an outlier'. For example, on reaching an income *per capita* equivalent to $550 (in 1970 US dollars) France in 1870 registered 49.3 per cent employed in agriculture and Britain (in 1840) 25.0 per cent, whilst the aggregate figure for nineteenth-century Europe was 54.6 per cent [97; 91; 26].

Secondly, if we turn to the industrial sector, there is the common assumption that the French were slow to take advantage of the new technologies and economies of scale normally associated with 'industrialization'. In 1981, Robert R. Locke conceded the revisionist point that French economic growth had been quite respectable, but he suggested that France had nonetheless fallen short in her industrialization, understood as the application of science and technology to production [74]. Once again, the case for the prosecution appears overwhelming. One could demonstrate that industry in France was conspicuously slow to cut its links with the agricultural world. Much of its early expansion during the eighteenth and early nineteenth centuries took place in the countryside. The same could be said of its British counterpart, of course, but in France (notably in the case of the handloom weavers) rural industry proved more resilient during the long rearguard action that followed against the factory system. One could also cite various indicators to measure levels of industrial development, which Bairoch has assembled to facilitate international comparisons. These will show, for example, that French industry had a relatively limited amount of steam power available to it. During the 1900s, fixed steam engines (which excludes those used in transport) produced the following horse-power per 1000 of population in the industrializing nations:

Germany	110
Belgium	150
USA	150
France	73
Italy	14
UK	220
Switzerland	37

Overall, Bairoch classifies France fifth among the European countries in her level of industrial development on the eve of the First World War [2]. One might also marshal evidence to suggest some preference in France for a small-scale form of industrial organization. During the nineteenth century an estimated nine-tenths of French manufacturing activity was in the framework of a *fabrique*: a network of specialized firms in a particular region producing goods by means of an extensive division of labour. These 'collective works' (to translate the untranslatable) were dominated by small and medium-sized enterprises, and included such diverse activities as weaving, lacemaking, mechanical engineering, building and food processing [57, *115*]. A census of 1906 provides more concrete evidence of an atomized industrial structure, with 3.7 million wage-earners working in no less than 600,000 'industrial establishments' (a term that will include butchers' and bakers' shops, it should be noted). One third of this labour force was to be found in establishments with less than ten workers, and the median was only 45 employees.

This is fine as far as it goes, but such an interpretation begs two questions. First, given that *all* European countries ended up with a 'dualistic' industrial structure at some point, in the sense that many small workshops survived and even flourished beside the larger ones, where did France come on the international spectrum? Unfortunately, problems of definition rule out the collection of reliable data to compare average plant or firm sizes in different countries [60, *161–70*]. Most authorities assert with some confidence that French industry was less concentrated than its major rivals – and, for what it is worth, a survey from 1962 would confirm this.[1] But they also stress the predominance of larger scale plants (over 100 workers) in certain branches of industry, notably chemicals, glass, textiles, paper and rubber. And in mining and metallurgy, where plants of over 500 workers accounted for approximately four-fifths of the labour force, concentration was more advanced than in Britain, though well behind that in the United States and Germany [15, IV, i, *258–64*; 1, *197–201*; 73, *5–7, 63–9*]. The second problem concerns the direction of causation. The relatively small scale of organization and associated technologies adopted by French industry could have been a handicap on the market, and hence a symptom of failure or retardation. Alternatively, as we shall see below, they could be interpreted as a successful adaptation to market conditions.

Finally, there is the unevenness of development across the regions to consider. Here at last there is a consensus among historians that these disparities were very marked in the French case during the eighteenth and nineteenth centuries. Drawing a line variously described as running from Cherbourg to Marseille or from Le Havre to Sète marks off a *France du développement* from a *France de la stagnation*. To the east lay regions of high cereals' yields and commercialized agriculture, dynamic industries, the main financial and commercial centres, easy communications and demographic progress. To the west, one finds a more dismal

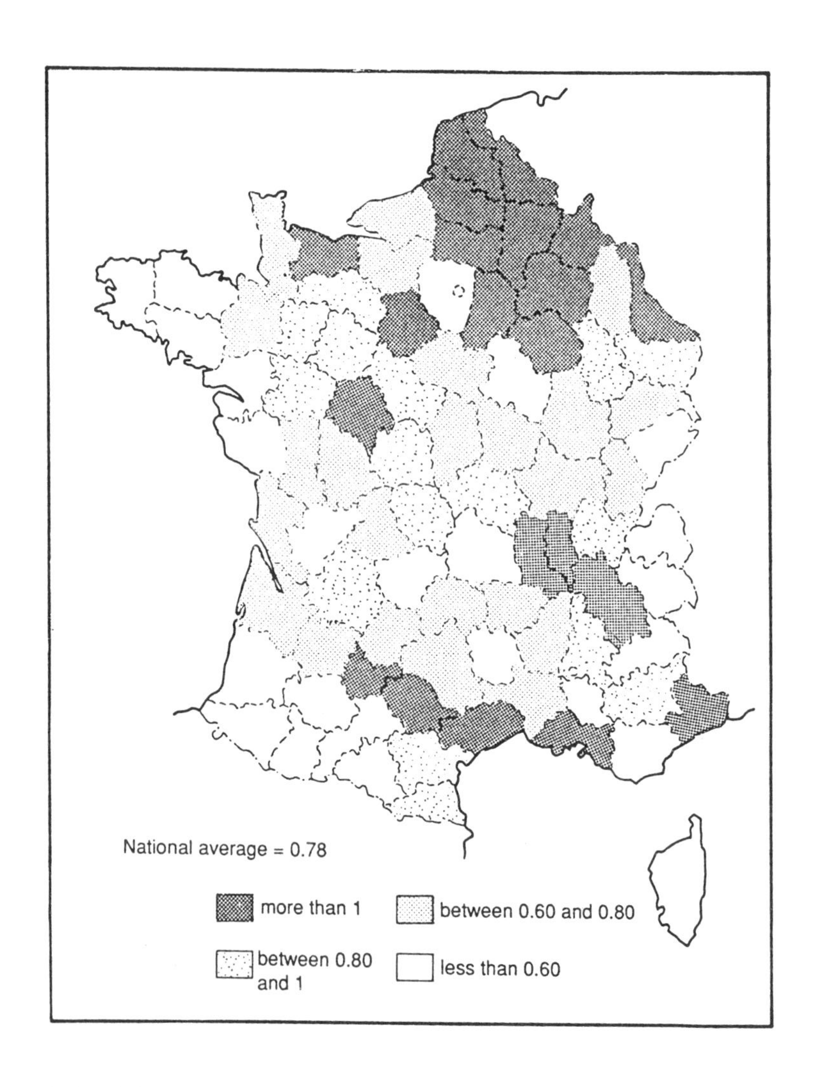

Industrial production per inhabitant (by department) 1910–12 (in thousands of francs)
Source: After A. Armengaud, *La Population française au XIXe siècle (PUF, 1971*).

pattern of archaic agriculture, declining industries, isolation and population losses. On the one side there was the Paris region, and the big industrial centres of Normandy, the Nord, Alsace-Lorraine and the Rhone valley. On the other there was the South, the South-East, the Massif and, most disadvantaged of all (in material terms), Brittany [15, IV, i, *315–42*]. A study by Toutain notes that such disparities (measured in terms of income per head of population) were deeply rooted in the French economy by the late eighteenth century. Although there would be some convergence between the 1860s and 1931, the gap would open again in the mid-twentieth century [103]. This leaves open a number of questions. First, given that in any country some areas are likely to develop more rapidly than others, would not a regional framework for analysis be more fruitful than a national one? Obviously this hardly suits our purpose here, but it stands as an interesting alternative perspective.[2] Secondly, were regional disparities greater in France than in, say Britain or Germany? Following on from that, did the French economy, as an aggregate, suffer more than its rivals from the burden of supporting a few very backward regions? We have no answers as yet.

Grasping the pattern of French economic development before 1914 proves remarkably difficult. At times, protagonists in the debate appear to stand at opposite, irreconcilable poles. 'The battered and tired French economy of the nineteenth century' berated by Trebilcock is a long way from 'one of the earliest and most successful cases of sustained modern industrial and economic growth' vaunted by Sewell [104, *197*; 101, *147*]. Yet the gradual, 'unobtrusive' path to industrialization which the revisionists have proposed is not too different from the 'sluggishness' that was common currency in the earlier literature. From the present perspective, two key points are worth emphasizing. First, if one assumes that international comparisons provide a useful yardstick by which to judge the French economic performance, then they should be based on a systematic compilation of data from as broad a range of developing countries as possible. Selective comparisons with, say, aspects of the British 'industrial revolution' or German and American industrialization in the late nineteenth century have proved misleading. The danger, of course, is to imply that one of these countries took an optimum path to development, and that France performed poorly insofar as she failed to follow suit. Second, the strengths as well as the weaknesses of French economic development should be recognized. Even the most dynamic economies, it should be remembered, must contend with forces resisting as well as forces promoting development, and have areas of comparative disadvantage as well as areas of comparative advantage. We have seen how the French performance is far from flattered when set against that of its rivals in a number of spheres. The level of her income *per capita* was always below that of the old enemy across the Channel, and even below those of some of her Continental neighbours. She could never have been described as an 'industrial giant': in 1913, Germany accounted for 14.8 per cent of world manufacturing output, the United Kingdom 13.6 per cent, France only 6.1 per cent [5, *296*]. And she did have to endure extended periods when 'stagnation' was much in evidence. At the same time, a sustained increase in *per capita* incomes that was of a similar order to those of the more developed economies in Europe stands out as the most important performance indicator for most purposes. It certainly paves the way for a sympathetic assessment of the various strategies adopted in France concerning the size of the agricultural sector, or the organization and technologies adopted by industrial enterprises. Overall, one can usefully cite Jean Bouvier, who concluded that French industrialization was regular, progressive, dualistic and without periods of marked acceleration [14, *17*].

3
Natural resources and the labour supply

Ideally our search for explanations of French economic growth before 1914 would begin with attempts to measure the contributions of its main determinants: rising inputs of natural resources, labour and capital, plus an increase in the productivity of these inputs. The reality is that economic historians have hesitated to give such a breakdown in the French case, partly for practical reasons of documentation, partly because of the marked discontinuities in the country's development [73, *10–11*]. This gap in the available data means that some imprecision is inevitable in what follows. Nonetheless, there is the consolation that estimates of 'total factor productivity' risk a spurious accuracy, raising as many questions as they answer. And, given certain uniformities of development among the advanced nations, it seems reasonable to assume that the sources of growth in France were broadly similar to those observed elsewhere. That is to say, the deeper we move into the nineteenth and twentieth centuries, the more growth in *per capita* output can be attributed to increases in the productivity of land, labour and capital, rather than to the deployment of greater quantities of these resources.[3] In this section we need to bear in mind two points. First, the empirical evidence (not to mention common sense) suggests that an increasing supply of natural resources was unlikely to be a major source of growth – though particular shortages in this field could result in important bottlenecks. Secondly, changes in the quality as well as the quantity of labour available could have important consequences for economic growth.

Most of the debates concerning natural resources in France have focused on the availability of minerals. Something of a consensus exists on a few basic points: that there was a problem with industrial raw materials; that there were ways of circumventing it; and that the French were not entirely successful in doing so. The main problem was a deficiency in coal. Unlike some of her neighbours, notably the Swiss and the Dutch, she was a substantial coal producer. Her output increased from 0.9 million tonnes in 1815 to 39.9 millions in 1910–13. But these figures pale in comparison with those for her two major rivals; at the same period, the British coal cut rose from 16.2 to 275.4 million tonnes, the German one from 1.2 to 247.5 million tonnes! French coal was apparently expensive to mine. Although methods of production were similar, pithead prices were on average 50 per cent higher than in the United Kingdom, and 20 per cent more than in Germany – or so the Comité des Forges would have had us believe [17, *8*]. To compound these drawbacks, the main coalfields in the Loire and the Nord were located a long distance from sources of iron ore, and from most industrial centres. During the 1840s, high transport costs meant that coal worth 15 francs per tonne at Saint-Etienne would cost 40 to 45 francs by the time it reached Paris. To get round the problem of high coal prices, various measures were adopted. Alternative sources of energy were used, particularly water and hydro-electric power. In Alsace, for example, as late as 1870, one fifth of the power used in cotton spinning and one third in cotton weaving came from water-wheels [49, *148*]. Coal-saving technology was introduced, such as high-pressure steam engines, mentioned in Alsace during the 1830s, or the re-use of waste gases from blast furnaces, attempted at Decazeville from 1835. Imports increased the supply of coal available and put pressure on domestic price levels. After 1870 they accounted for approximately one third of total consumption. Finally, and most importantly, transport improvements brought dramatic reductions in the cost of coal for industrialists. Canal and railway construction meant that the average price of a tonne of coal in the Haut-Rhin Department fell from 40 francs in 1838 to 23.7 francs in 1867.

Some authorities consider that more could have been done to solve the fuel problem. They note the relative slowness to invest in the transport infrastructure, and the levying of tariffs on imported coal at various points between 1819 and 1910. The tariff could always be seen as a part of an attempt by Governments to balance the interests of domestic producers and consumers, in the context of an energy deficit. In the long run, so the argument goes, the economy would benefit as some form of protection encouraged investment in mining and transportation [43, *20*]. But for the critics it was 'neither necessary nor wise' in a country reputedly deprived of coal [104, *170*]. Ultimately more important, however, is the question of whether high coal prices had a significant impact on industrial development. On the one hand, it could be pointed out that France was the only major developing economy to remain dependent on coal imports, and that high prices were a permanent national handicap [1, *101–3*]. Had a 'bountiful nature' given her substantially larger deposits of easily-mined coal, she would undoubtedly have been able to generate more in the way of employment, incomes and exports. On the other hand, there is the contention that the high price of coal was simply a challenge that invited an appropriate response, meaning that it was not a fundamental obstacle to development [60, *15–29;* 104, *167–73*]. Certainly there is no disputing that in a modern, industrializing economy, natural resources will not be a determining influence; humanity is no longer tied to nature. It is also generally recognized that shortages of a particular factor can be a stimulus to technical progress and, conversely, an abundance can be a source of inertia. Ironically, a more acute shortage of timber in Britain than in France during the eighteenth and early nineteenth centuries may account for the earlier diffusion of coke-smelting in British ironworks [30, *37–9*].

Yet the drawback of high coal prices cannot be discounted entirely, bearing in mind a varying impact over time and between different industries. The problem was particularly acute before the opening up of the Northern coalfield and investment in the transport infrastructure eased the burden from the 1830s. It also affected 'heat-intensive' industries, such as basic metallurgy and glassmaking, more than, say, textiles. A study of production costs in the iron industries of Western Europe during the 1850s reveals 'extremely high French values' for fuel costs: around 60 per cent of variable costs, compared to 44 per cent in Cleveland, 30 per cent in Dusseldorf and 18 per cent in South Wales [38, *163*]. The upshot, as Lévy-Leboyer revealed some time ago, was to encourage French specialization in finished goods rather than semi-manufactures, in labour- rather than energy-intensive forms of production [67; 68].

Turning now to the supply of labour in France, one finds the literature riddled with paradoxes. This factor of production is depicted as both a source of strength and a source of weakness. During the eighteenth and early nineteenth centuries, an abundance of labour in France has been identified as an obstacle to development. Yet less than a hundred years later it was supposedly a shortage that was causing problems. Similarly, the French economy can be shown to have benefited from the skills and good taste for which sections of its labour force were renowned worldwide. Yet the very success in cultivating traditional craft skills may in its turn have been a handicap, in so far as the French 'culture of production' was ill-adapted to the new age of steam and mechanization. Finally, there is the rather odd phenomenon of a labour force that was both weakly unionized and fearsome in its militancy, from the insurrectionary silk-weavers of Lyon in the 1830s, to the revolutionary syndicalists of Paris in the 1900s.

To take first the shift from a relative abundance of labour to a relative shortage in the French economy, the middle of the nineteenth century stands out as an important turning point. Before then, the evidence suggests that there existed a constantly swelling reservoir of cheap and often underemployed labour in both rural and urban areas. The underlying influence here was the increasing pressure of population on resources. Demographic growth in France may have been subdued by contemporary European standards (a 39 per cent increase between 1680 and 1830, compared to 133 per cent in England), but in a country already verging on overpopulation in the seventeenth century, the impact on the labour market was dramatic [37]. No doubt there were often shortages of particular types of labour (notably the skilled labour required in developing industries such as cotton spinning and machine construction) and in the short term certain periods experienced difficulties (above all, the period of the Revolutionary and Napoleonic Wars). But more in evidence were the symptoms of an overcrowded labour market, such as hordes of rootless beggars and 'vagabonds' on the roads, a network of seasonal migrations, declining or stagnant real wages, and widespread poverty. One recent study submits that this 'surplus of still underemployed manpower' continued into the twentieth century, on the grounds that reserves of labour were never scarce during periods of rapid growth [73, *69*, *297–9*]. A more widely-held view would see some tightening of the labour market from the 1850s and 1860s onwards [20]. The underlying reason was a peculiarly French slackening in the rate of population increase at this point, which coincided with a growing demand for labour as the economy diversified. A chorus of complaints came from the land, beginning in the Paris region, the North-East and the South-East around Marseille, areas where farmers had to compete with industry and commerce [93]. Meanwhile, employers in heavy industry (mining, iron and steel, chemicals) often faced their own problems in recruiting workers. Around 1900, for example, the rapidly-expanding steelworks of Longwy, in Lorraine, first experienced difficulties in mobilizing large numbers of semi-skilled workers [86, *68*]. Overall, the quantitative evidence suggests a sustained increase in the French labour supply, but a modest one by international standards. O'Brien and Keyder estimate that the labour force employed in commodity production (which covers the numbers employed, but makes no allowance for average hours worked) rose from 8 million in 1803–12 to 14.9 million in 1905–13. We should bear in mind here that 'the construction of workforce series poses numerous problems and, given the actual state of the documentation, it is difficult to see how they could be resolved' [73, *293*]. Not surprisingly, then, the sources on which these figures are based have been challenged by Crafts [26, *62–5*]. Nonetheless, they may not be far wide of the mark in showing that while the French labour force almost doubled in size during the nineteenth century, its British counterpart nearly tripled [91, *86*].

How important, then, was this ebb and flow in the labour supply for overall economic development? Crouzet has been influential in assigning it a major role during the eighteenth century. He asserts that 'the most important of the differences to be observed between England and France' was the shortage of labour in England, which provided a strong incentive to invent and take up labour-saving machinery, compared to the vast reserves of labour in France, which allowed output to be increased without 'drastic innovations' [30, *39–41*, *90–3*]. At first sight, Crouzet might appear perverse in highlighting as a weakness one area where France enjoyed a clear comparative advantage over England: low wages. French entrepreneurs benefited from the vast reserves of cheap labour to be found in the French countryside, much of which was accustomed to doing part-time industrial work. Cheap labour could also be deployed to good advantage in the factory system. Lévy-Leboyer cites evidence from an enquiry in the 1830s concerning cotton-spinning. It contended that a British operative was responsible for two machines with 620 spindles, producing 125 kilogrammes of spun cotton per week. His counterpart in Alsace was reported to have only one machine, with 366 spindles. But he worked for 84 hours a week, 15 hours more than the British equivalent, and he could produce 90 kilogrammes for half the wage [67, *90*]. More generally, Lévy-Leboyer concludes that British and French industrialization proceeded along complementary lines, the two economies simply using to the full the factors of production available – in the one case capital, in the other labour [68, *292*]. Yet cheap labour was never a panacea for French employers. There was always the risk of being undercut by even lower wage levels further east in Europe: competition from the German states in particular loomed large. And Crouzet is surely correct in identifying the abundance of labour as an important factor in explaining the leisurely pace of French economic development: it permitted growth to be sustained within slowly-evolving industrial structures.

As for the labour shortages appearing towards the end of our period, they have sometimes been depicted as a serious bottleneck. To quote Clive Trebilcock, 'the snagged development of the French economy may have followed simply from a lack of Frenchmen' [104, *164*]. That labour recruitment was a constant struggle for many enterprises is not in dispute. Nor is there any doubt that attempts at long-distance recruitment, to supplement the local sources of labour on which most employers could rely, never gained any real momentum. The mines at La Grande-Combe, in the Gard, have become notorious for their largely futile attempts to attract workers from outside the region, foraging as far afield as Piedmont, the Forez, Burgundy, and Rouen (among redundant cotton workers in 1862!). Such admissions do not rule out the possibility that labour shortages were never a serious hurdle for economic development. As Kindleberger put it, 'The condition is interesting, but it explains little' [60, *238*]. Various remedies were available for the 'condition'. First, females, and particularly married women, could be employed in large numbers to boost participation rates. In 1901, 40 per cent of French women were considered to be economically active, compared to only 10 per cent in Britain and Germany. The small farms of the peasantry readily mobilized (and exploited) family labour, and so too did the smaller workshops in industry. In the towns and villages of the Lyonnais, for example, women workers were reported to be playing an increasingly important role after 1850 in the various branches of handloom weaving, ribbon and braid making, and the manufacture of gloves [65, I, *135–6*]. Secondly, peasant-workers could be brought in daily from a wider area by train, as in the northern coalfields. Thirdly, foreign labour could be drafted in on a large scale, attracted by relatively high wages in the more developed regions of France. At a time when many European countries were losing emigrants to North America and elsewhere, France once again stood out with its heavy balance of immigrants. Before the 1880s, the main flows were from Belgium and Germany; later it was Italians and Spaniards who predominated. Immigrants became indispensable for certain industries, notably metallurgy (17.8 per cent of its workers in 1906), chemicals and construction. For example, the mines and steelworks of Decazeville turned to northern Spain for their unskilled labourers in the early twentieth century. Meanwhile the mushrooming steel towns of Lorraine became a veritable Tower of Babel at this same period, with their contingents of Belgians, Italians, Germans, Poles and even North Africans [28, *20–4*; 96, *119*; 86, *165–72*; 88, *97–102*]. Finally, to go on to a rather different tack, various measures could be taken to increase both the quality and quantity of effort and skill forthcoming from workers.

This latter dimension to the labour supply brings us to qualitative as opposed to quantitative changes during the course of development. Here another of the great strengths of the French economy comes into focus. Not only did France have a very large population (32.6 million in 1831, compared to 28.2 million in the German states and 16.3 million in Great Britain): she also had one that was renowned for its craftsmanship. Communities of craftsmen and women in the *fabriques* harboured the secrets of their trade over the generations maintaining a favourable environment for the production of fashion and luxury goods. Examples are legion: the cabinetmakers of the Faubourg Saint-Antoine in Paris, the silkweavers of Lyon, the armourers of Saint-Etienne, the lacemakers of Valenciennes – and later on the manufacturers of cars and aeroplanes in a number of cities [57, *74*]. On the other side of the coin, though, French workers have a fearsome reputation for rebelling against the factory system. One could point to their long struggle against mechanization during the first half of the nineteenth century; their long-standing links with agriculture; and their militancy during the strike waves of the late nineteenth and early twentieth centuries. And if their formal organization was limited (only 8.4 per cent of labour was unionized as late as 1911), French workers were ruthless in wielding informal methods of resistance to the demands made on them by employers. They were prepared to withdraw their labour individually, to argue with overseers, or to work as slowly as possible [92; 57, *72–83, 111–53*]. But was this ever a serious obstacle to industrial development in nineteenth century France?

It seems unlikely. French historians would do well to remember that all developing economies face the problem of resistance from labour to the new industrial discipline, and all must take steps to train and motivate a factory proletariat. Whether French workers can be described as exceptionally recalcitrant remains an open question, and one which perhaps can never be resolved definitively. Either way, there are certain indicators that, like their counterparts elsewhere, they could be 'persuaded' to adapt to the skills and commitment to industrial work required by large-scale industry. Literacy rates increased from an unimpressive 47 per cent of men and 27 per cent of women signing their marriage registers on the eve of the French Revolution, to a more creditable 78 per cent of men and 66 per cent of women signing in the early 1870s. Industrial skills were learned on the job, as the traditional apprenticeship system was moulded to the needs of the factory system. Loyalty to a particular firm could be encouraged by various welfare schemes, such as plots of land, subsidized housing, canteens, shops, and pension schemes. More ambitiously, in the hope of engendering an improved 'morality of productive labour', some companies founded schools, libraries, churches and recreational associations. (This at least was the model, implemented in famous cases like the *indiennages* in and around Mulhouse or the Le Creusot ironworks: the majority of smaller enterprises never came close to it) [92; 96; 87]. During the early twentieth century, there was even a hint of scientific labour management appearing on the shop floor, with efforts to devise sophisticated systems of bonus payments [39]. The record of individual firms in reducing labour turnover or avoiding strikes could be impressive. At the Saint-Gobain glassworks, for example, second to none in its paternalistic efforts, half of the employees had more than ten years of service with the company in 1900, and 'good behaviour' always prevailed on the shop floor [33, *369–79*].

The final, acid test to apply is to look at data on labour productivity in French industry. The case has been made that the productivity of labour in French industry was above British levels during the nineteenth century. O'Brien and Keyder ruffled plenty of feathers in the historical profession when they made this claim in 1978. They observed at the outset:

> Historians might be willing to accept the superior productivity of labour employed in French industry before the Revolution. But few will readily believe in statistics which indicate that output per worker in French industry as a whole remained above British levels throughout the Industrial Revolution and that the British 'lag' (while diminishing steadily in relative terms) persisted into the 1890s.
> [91, *146*]

And, needless to say, few did. A recent reworking of the evidence by Crafts somewhat predictably concludes that labour productivity in French industry was generally a little below the British level. It goes on to assert that the growth of industrial productivity in France during the late nineteenth century may have matched the British performance, but it was much slower than the German one [26, *60–6*]. Yet even if we accept that the French performance was, as ever, merely 'respectable', it is interesting to consider further material assembled by O'Brien and Keyder on the product mix in Britain and France during the period 1905–13. On the one hand, this shows British labour productivity to have been higher than the French in mining, iron and steel, shipbuilding, chemicals and glass. These were fuel-intensive industries, and so it seems likely that the figures are influenced by British advantages in the location and accessibility of coal. On the other hand, the productivity of labour in certain 'new' industries – rubber, electricity and petroleum – was higher in France, indicating some success in responding to the challenge of large-scale production. No less importantly, the same pattern of superior French labour productivity also emerges in several of the smaller-scale industries, notably construction, leather articles, clothing and hosiery. The authors go on to note that 'about 75 per cent of the French industrial labour force found work in industries where value added per employee was either equal to or above levels obtained in comparable British industries'. Hence they conclude that comparative advantage and market forces combined to produce complementary industrial structures, the British excelling in a few basic industries, the French in the finishing end of manufacturing. It follows that French industry was 'different' rather than 'backward' compared to the British [91, *151–60*]. In this perspective, the contention must be that if French labour had some preference for skilled work in small workshops, this was less an obstacle to French industrialization, more an influence on the particular path it took.

4
Capital and technical progress

Let us return for a moment to the assertion from Lévy-Leboyer that during the course of their industrialization the French and British economies 'simply made maximum use of the factors of production available – in the one case labour, in the other capital' [68, *292*]. This implies that if the labour supply was a source of strength in France, capital was something of a weakness. There was indeed a time when the early start made by the British on the path of industrialization was attributed to an abundance of capital. Economic theory appeared to justify this interpretation, with models in which the rate of growth of output was determined by the level of investment. A common assertion was that a vital difference between 'preindustrial' and industrial economies was that the former saved and invested 4 or 5 per cent of national income, the latter a minimum of 12 to 15 per cent. But in the French case, econometricians have noted a disconcerting decline in the investment ratio during the late nineteenth century. A recent estimate shows the share of national product invested at home falling from 12.0 per cent in 1850–59 to 11.7 per cent in 1879 – and doing much the same again between the 1880s and the 1890s [79, *239*]. A promising explanation for French 'stagnation' looms on the horizon ... However, another school of thought in economics countered by playing down the role of capital formation in economic growth, emphasizing instead the overwhelming impact of technical progress. Investment might then appear more a consequence than a cause of growth. The key influences on the French pattern of development would then have to be sought elsewhere. The fact remains that some historians have persisted in giving a prominent role to aspects of capital formation in France.

And, given that the influence of technical progress can only be measured as a 'residual', there is a risk of underestimating that of capital. Most importantly, 'the productivity opportunities offered by technical progress cannot be exploited unless the capital stock per worker is renewed and expanded' [75, *109*].

Capital formation involves three activities: saving, which sets aside resources from current consumption; finance, which seeks to bridge the gap between savers and investors; and investment, which involves the commitment of resources to the production of capital goods.[4] Historians have found it difficult to decide whether the first activity was adequately fulfilled in the French case. Lévy-Leboyer notes that revolution and war during the 1790s may have impoverished a generation of savers, and that the level of savings stagnated during the third quarter of the nineteenth century [67, *417*; 73, *23*]. In general, though, the various authorities have tended to assume a large enough pool of savings for development [60, *39–40*; 17, *113*]. This appears plausible in a nation with a long commercial tradition and relatively high incomes by 1750. The real conundrums arise with the second activity, that is to say in the financial sector of the economy. Everyone agrees that banks and other financial institutions can only operate where a demand for their services exists. Their role is not to create capital, but to guide national and foreign savings to expanding sectors. Hence they are fundamentally dependant on the level of economic development around them. But historians are reluctant to accept a purely passive role for them. The problem then is to decide how large the 'margin of liberty' they enjoy in an economy might be, and whether they use it to exert a positive, neutral or negative influence on overall development. At one extreme stand authors who argue that 'France lagged a hundred years behind Britain in money, banking and finance, and that this was both a reflection and a cause of its economic retardation' [61, *115*; 18]. At the other is Lévy-Leboyer. He asserts that by the 1840s the financial market gave the impression of being the dynamic part of the economy, contributing to a growth rate of industrial output and exports that was 'honourable' when compared to the British performance [67, *409*, *699*].

Consideration of two, more specific, questions will help us to judge these issues. Was the financial sector unduly cautious in its dealings with industry? And did it harm domestic interests by draining off capital abroad? At first sight, the French banking system appears to have fallen between two stools. On the one hand, it was slow to follow the British in developing a range of specialized institutions. As Cameron observes, France entered the nineteenth century with virtually a clean slate in this sphere [18, *101*]. In the background lay the murky activities of John Law: the bursting of his 'Mississippi Bubble' in 1720 may have set back the cause of banks and banking in France by a century [61, *96*]. Various initiatives were taken from the Napoleonic period onwards, but in the middle of the nineteenth century, Cameron concludes that France had an inadequate number and distribution of bank offices, and an insufficient variety of specialized financial institutions [18, *127*]. On the other hand, between 1850 and 1880 France helped pioneer 'la grande banque à tout faire', the mixed bank typical of Continental Europe, but she did not persist with it to a maturer stage. A number of bankers were inspired by the Saint-Simonian vision of a huge institution that would collect the savings of the masses and use them to finance industrial expansion. The best known examples are the Pereire brothers and their Crédit Mobilier of 1852. They engaged in a ruthless struggle with the Rothschild family, reminiscent of a Mafia war, to secure foreign loans and railway concessions. But the new joint-stock banks soon learnt that they could easily burn their fingers handling long-term industrial investments. Consequently, from the 1880s they became deposit banks, restricting themselves to short-term commercial transactions – and to speculation in foreign bonds. This pattern of development may have placed French industry, and capital-intensive industries such as iron and steel in particular, at a disadvantage compared to foreign rivals [82]. Alternatively, entrepreneurs in France (taking on the third activity of investment) may have made few demands on the financial sector. In the early stages of industrialization, capital to launch an enterprise was raised informally, among family, friends and neighbours. The case of Alsace illustrates the relatively low cost of buildings and machinery during the early nineteenth century. In the Bas-Rhin department, somewhere between 10,000 and 50,000 francs (£400–£2000) would have been sufficient for all but a handful of industrial firms. Such sums were well within the capacity of the local bourgeoisie: textile manufacturers came from families of merchants, dyers, pharmacists, hoteliers and the like [49, *327–35*]. When it came to the later stages of expansion, nearly all firms across the country relied on retained profits. To take one particularly striking example from many, between 1702 and 1920 the Saint-Gobain glass and chemical company never once solicited its shareholders for additional capital, preferring to draw on its own reserves [33, *90–1*].

Our inclination here is to follow Jean Bouvier in assigning the banking system a small rather than a large 'margin of liberty', and in doubting that it exhibited any significant 'lag' [12; 13]. Thus if the banking network was somewhat patchy until the late nineteenth century, this may simply reflect the uneven distribution of manufacturing and trading activities across the regions. And if the banks tended to confine themselves to short-term operations, this may have been because the demand from industry was principally for working (as opposed to fixed) capital and for emergency support during a crisis. They were not necessarily unresponsive to demands for longer-term commitments either. From the outset, heavy industry had often been obliged to turn to the financial markets for venture capital. The Anzin coalmining company was half-owned by a consortium of Parisian private bankers from 1795 when it had to be repurchased from the state. Similarly, in 1811 the ironmaster François de Wendel turned to the Seillière bank in Nancy for a loan of 300,000 francs, part of which was repaid, the rest entering the bank's portfolio [42; 106]. At a later stage of industrialization, vast amounts of capital had to be mobilized to support investment in the infrastructure and capital-intensive 'new' industries. This provided opportunities from the 1850s for Crédit Mobilier-type banks, a handful of *banques d'affaires* (investment banks), and the stock markets, not to mention a host of local and regional banks. But the openings were first exploited during the first half of the century by the supposedly conservative and exclusive *haute banque* in Paris [67]. We venture to suggest that entrepreneurs in France experienced no more difficulties than their competitors in the search for venture capital, and that the system of banks and credit was appropriate to prevailing conditions in France [79, *363–73*].

But what of the massive export of capital from France during the nineteenth century? Table 4.1 makes it clear that France was

Table 4.1 *Growth of foreign investments of selected leading capital-exporting countries (in millions of US dollars)*

Country	1825	1855	1870	1885	1900	1915
United Kingdom	500	2300	4900	7800	12,100	19,500
France	100	1000	2500	3300	5200	8600
Germany	—	—	—	1900	4800	6700
Netherlands	300	300	500	1000	1100	1200

Source: W. Woodruff, *Impact of Western Man* (London, 1966), p. 150.

second only to Britain in this field – even if a distant second. During the 1880s, the average annual income from loans and investments abroad probably accounted for 2 per cent of the national income; by 1914, it was close to 6 per cent. Right from the start, there was a heated debate over whether such massive outflows of capital helped or hindered the development of the economy. For *aficionados* of conspiracy theories, there is the thesis that politicians, bankers and a corrupt financial press combined to persuade savers to invest in sectors that were relatively unproductive for the French economy. On the one side stood a Republic desperate to find allies for the inevitable struggle against Germany, to the extent that it would buy influence abroad. All too ready to support it were the banks, efficiently 'draining' French savings out of the country, and financial journalists, writing for political paymasters at home and abroad. On the other side was a mass of small savers who found foreign government bonds much to their taste: over half of French capital exports took this form, notably to shaky autocratic régimes such as Russia (which was fine, until 1917 . . .), Turkey and Egypt. The alleged result was that these *rentier* type of capitalists, contentedly sitting at home clipping their coupons, starved French industry of venture capital, and did little to generate foreign trade. A close look at the evidence makes this line of argument difficult to sustain. In the first place, the chronology of events is all wrong. Surges of foreign investment tended to coincide with periods of prosperity at home, as in the mid-nineteenth and early twentieth centuries, whilst years of weak foreign investment coincided with domestic stagnation, as between 1882 and 1897. This might suggest that external investments boosted growth, by generating resources in foreign markets. (The predominance of loans to governments abroad should not be allowed to obscure a growing role for shareholdings in foreign companies from the 1890s.) In the second place, as Lévy-Leboyer shows, the potential for foreign investments to stimulate exports was strictly limited by the late nineteenth century. France was most successful at exporting consumer goods to relatively affluent countries, which had little demand for French capital. Conversely, her producer goods were generally uncompetitive, making little headway in the less developed countries which sought her capital. Finally, French interest rates were, on average, low: in 1905–13 the discount rate was 2.7 per cent in Paris, compared to 3.3 per cent in London. Hence the conclusion that even if the export of capital might be deemed 'excessive', it could hardly have done much to deprive French industry of funds [60, *58*; 70; 73].

This leaves us with technical progress, by far the most elusive of all the influences on economic growth. The usual practice has been to identify it with the 'residual' left when the contribution of the physical inputs of land, labour and capital have been taken into account. But any such estimate includes a whole range of other growth factors, such as economies of scale and improvements in the quality of labour, making it a 'measure of our ignorance' as much as anything else.[5] An alternative 'rough proxy measure' of the pace of technical progress proposed by Maddison is the growth rate of labour productivity. International comparisons reveal that this indicator tends to mirror those measuring the overall performance of an economy. Hence during the period 1870 to 1913 the growth of French GDP per man-hour was above average for the developed countries at 1.8 per cent a year (compared to 1.9 per cent in Germany and 1.2 per cent in the United Kingdom). But the level of labour productivity was less impressive. In 1913 France and Germany could manage only 54 and 57 per cent respectively of productivity levels in the United States, compared to 81 per cent in the United Kingdom [75, *96–102*]. As might be expected, such ambivalent figures can be interpreted in a number of ways. The key question is whether they reflect more the obstacles to the diffusion of new technology in France, or a moderately successful adaptation of technology to prevailing circumstances.

Certain preliminary points have proved uncontentious. In the first place, the French had a rather patchy record as inventors, their successes being largely confined to textiles and chemicals (the Leblanc soda process, Heilmann's woolcombing machine, Chardonnet's artificial silk, for example). Industrialists therefore had to rely heavily on foreign technology, and above all the long series of British inventions from the Industrial Revolution period. Secondly, historians now recognize that the process of transferring technologies between countries is likely to be a slow one. Innovations must be adapted to local factor prices, resource endowments, consumer tastes, labour relations and so on [75, *108*]. Yet during this period of assimilation there is always the risk that entrepreneurs will be cut off from the latest developments in the lead country, as happened during the long sequence of Revolutionary and Napoleonic Wars between 1792 and 1815. There was too the arduous business of learning by trial-and-error a range of new management and labour skills. John Harris has been influential in emphasizing French problems in assimilating 'coal-fuel technology'. In his own words, 'These apparently secondary, even menial, skills I am sure account for much of the difficulty in exporting British technologies, and this was particularly serious in the knowledge of coking-coals and how to produce suitable cokes' [47, *7*]. The most strategically-important example was the slow diffusion of coke-smelting techniques in the iron industry. Experiments with producing coke blast iron were begun at Le Creusot in 1785, but thirty years later, despite an ample harvest of information, French producers still lacked the detailed, concrete knowledge that would allow them to make any headway [106, *316*; 48]. Similar examples could be cited in metalworking, glass, pottery and the dyeing and finishing of textiles.

Where historians diverge is in their assessment of this process of adaptation. On the one hand, French industry can be depicted struggling to catch up with its British rival, as a huge 'technical lag' opened up during the late eighteenth and early nineteenth centuries [30, *26–7*, *344*]. For historians who argue that the performance of the French economy should be judged in terms of its shift to capital-intensive, technologically progressive forms of industry (as opposed to its growth), such a gap provides conclusive evidence of a retarded economy. 'French industrial performance has been judged marginally, against that of the most advanced industrial countries, and has been found wanting' [74, *430*]. On the other hand, O'Brien and Keyder suggest that this picture of a technological race between leaders and 'also rans' is misleading. They tend to play down lags in the initial adoption of new technology, and conclude that 'techniques used in France may have been more or less in line with factor prices' [91, *192*].

From our earlier examination of the factor endowment, it might be gauged that labour-saving and energy-using technology would be less attractive to French than to British entrepreneurs for much of our period. The importance of the overall economic context for entrepreneurial decisions on new technology can be readily understood if we return to the case of the iron industry. During the early nineteenth century, as Harris emphasizes, the incentive for French ironmasters to persist in trying to learn the technique of coke-smelting in a relatively short space of time was weakened by the acceptable level of charcoal costs, the difficulties of access to coal and the scope for meeting the growth in national demand with charcoal pig [48, *39*].

A closer look at two significant characteristics of French development will reveal both strengths and weaknesses on the technical side. First, there was the massive expansion of industry in the countryside. This involved a low level of technology and a small scale of production: handtool methods used in domestic workshops for the most part, as in the handloom weaving industries of Normandy and the Lyonnais, or metalworking around Saint-Etienne. Proto-industrialization theory allows a dynamic rule for these rural handicrafts in the development of an economy, laying the foundations for industrialization proper. It also indicates why cottage industry was so admirably suited to French conditions. Hard-pressed peasant households were relieved to find an occupation that would tide them over the 'dead' season in agriculture, and help compensate for either the excessive division of landholdings (as in parts of Alsace and Flanders) or the precarious existence of small tenant farmers and agricultural labourers (as in the Pays de Caux) [46]. Merchant-manufacturers for their part were eager to exploit a labour force that was cheap, pliant and able to survive when laid off during a commercial crisis. This form of industrial organization proved remarkably resilient in France. Small-scale charcoal smelters continued to flourish in the iron industries of Lorraine, the Champagne, the Forez and the Ariège until the middle of the nineteenth century; and handloom weaving continued to expand right up until the 1870s. Yet there was always the risk that a region would become trapped for decades in a semi-backward state. The *champagne pouilleuse* ('the dusty Champagne') around Troyes was an area of poor soil and subdivided property whose impoverished population desperately turned to framework knitting in the late eighteenth century. But eventually the job opportunities provided by the hosiery industry fixed peasants on the land, encouraged large families and even attracted immigrants. By the 1840s, a vicious circle of low wages and stagnant technology had taken hold. Also, as Locke is keen to emphasize, however thriving the proto-industrial economy might be, at some stage in the nineteenth century the transition would have to be made to a more scientifically and technologically dynamic economy [74, *429*].

A second industrial strategy involved mechanizing handicraft production. France, in contrast to the United States, and, to a lesser extent, Britain, has been described by Charles Sabel as a centre for 'flexible specialization'.[6] The aim was to develop increasingly sophisticated versions of artisan tools, for use by skilled labour on a wide range of manufacturing tasks. The best-known example is the Jacquard loom, perfected in Lyon between 1800 and 1820: its 'silent technological revolution' introduced a system of perforated cards that reduced the cost of hand weaving fancy brocaded silks. Other examples can be found within the factory system. In the calico-printing works of Alsace, mechanization in the form of roller printing was gradually introduced from the early nineteenth century. But the machinery still made heavy demands on the skills of the operative, since printing on cloth, which could expand and contract, and printing with colours to satisfy various types of market, was far more difficult than printing on paper. This 'skill-intensive' form of industrialization had a number of advantages. It was well suited to the craft traditions of French labour. Its emphasis on quality and diversity was appropriate to a country with highly differentiated regional markets. And it had a forward-looking, creative side: by constantly varying the assortment of goods on offer, French producers sought out new markets at home and abroad. Its many small firms were particularly adept at responding to and encouraging rapid changes in demand. The world of fashion provides an obvious example, where Lyonese silks, fancy woollens from Roubaix and clothes made in Paris were conspicuously successful.

The question mark that hangs over 'flexible specialization' is the extent to which it could displace its obvious rival: mass production for mass markets. It is possible that historians have been as dazzled by the new assembly-line techniques associated with the name of Henry Ford as contemporary observers allegedly were. But they are often less impressed by the 'technological vitality' of French industry than Sabel and his colleagues.[7] Pierre Cayez, who is frequently cited by Sabel, depicts the Lyon silk industry gradually succumbing to overseas competition in the late nineteenth century: 'An ancient industry, partially paralysed by the weight of the past, had to take on newer industries, that were often created on an industrial rather than an artisanal base, and so were better equipped' [21, *19–22*]. Similarly, in the case of the car industry, Patrick Fridenson accepts that France was superb at running a labour-intensive, quasi-artisanal type of production. But on the eve of the First World War he points to shadows looming, in the form of American competition, and argues that France was slow to concentrate production and introduce standardized, interchangeable parts [39]. It might be added that many trades were only lightly touched by some form of 'flexible specialization'. In nineteenth-century Paris, for example, the artisan sector reinvigorated itself with various new techniques, including sewing machines, power saws and improved dyestuffs. But an increasing sub-division of tasks also caused some 'de-skilling' of labour. In 1910 the clothing industry employed 650,000 women outworkers, who earned in a day what a Renault mechanic earned in an hour. Such an unequal distribution of incomes acted as a drag on industrial consumption, and hence on growth itself [73, *72*].

Overall, if we think of the factor endowment as the cards which business leaders had to play, the impression is of a mixed hand. They had plenty of water-power but modest coal deposits; they faced a labour force which preferred working with handtools to a machine; and they were served by a financial sector that was poorly-developed until the 'banking revolution' of the mid-nineteenth century. They could of course augment their hand, with for example imported coal or immigrant workers – and they did so extensively. Moreover, unlike a card player, they could increase the productivity of their assets with various forms of technical progress. It follows that deficiencies in any particular area need not be a permanent handicap. At the same time, entrepreneurs were bound to adapt to their areas of comparative advantage and disadvantage. Two major influences stand out. First, there was the problem with coal supplies, which appears to be making a comeback as a major influence on the industrialization of various regions in Europe. This caused some weakness in basic industries such as iron and steel, and encouraged the location of industry in the countryside. Secondly, there was the abundance of cheap, craft-orientated labour. Here the pressure was towards labour- rather than capital-intensive forms of production, and to short-production runs of high-quality goods rather than to long runs of cheap, mass-produced items. Our conclusion would be that the technological and organizational forms adopted by French industry were generally well adapted to relative factor costs and the aptitudes of French labour. However, for a fuller understanding of these strategies, we must look beyond industry, to the agricultural and commercial sectors.

5
An agricultural revolution?

What is required from agriculture during the course of industrialization is an increase in productivity. This allows the primary sector to meet the inevitable rise in demand for food and industrial materials, and also to 'release' resources (principally labour and capital) to industry and the services. The 'revolutionary' measures that would make possible higher productivity took two forms. First, there was the diffusion of new techniques for cultivating the soil: the advanced crop rotations and heavier stocking of animals that permitted an intensification of mixed husbandry, and later, after about 1840, chemical fertilisers and farm machinery. Second, there were organizational changes, notably enclosures and the consolidation of holdings. So gradual was this revolution in France that historians have had great difficulty in pinning down its progress. Yet the chronology of change is of critical importance in the debates surrounding French agriculture. Three key questions have to be confronted when assessing the responsiveness of French agriculture to change. When did productivity on the land begin to rise? What was the influence of the system of land tenure? And what role did agriculture play in overall development?

At one extreme, an early start to the agricultural revolution would be consistent with a strong or 'propulsive role' for the primary sector in the development process. Bairoch champions the thesis that profound changes in the system of agriculture would be necessary *before* any industrial revolution could take place [24, *452–506*]. The logic here is that without a prior increase in agricultural productivity, industrialization would risk grinding to a halt with a series of famines. Bairoch originally suggested the 1750s as the approximate date for the beginnings of an agricultural revolution in France, although he has since revised this to the slightly later period 1790 to 1820. Statistical evidence assembled by J.-C. Toutain for the *Histoire quantitative* also points to significant change on the land during the eighteenth century. Between 1701–10 and 1781–90 Toutain estimates that there was a 60 per cent increase in the 'final deflated agricultural product', which comfortably outstripped the 28 per cent increase in population, and suggests an end to the massive famines of the past. However, this line of argument provoked a series of ferocious counterblasts from other historians, calling into question both the data and the general thesis proposed by Bairoch [1, *27–52*].

Michel Morineau accuses Bairoch of being an economist who uses history as an arsenal without first checking his powder [83]. His own very striking conclusion is that as late as 1840, well after the beginnings of overall development in the French economy, there was no sign of an agricultural revolution. Morineau disputes the value of national averages in this field, preferring instead a regional framework. He concentrates on crop yields, particularly for cereals, using an official enquiry of 1840 to show the familiar disparity between departments north and south of the River Loire. Two southern departments, the Lozère and the Loire, are shown to produce a 'Medieval' yield of 3.8 to 1 on wheat seeds; the majority were below a ratio of 6 to 1. Only the Nord and the Pas-de-Calais could stand comparison with the advanced agricultures of England, Holland and Belgium. But what of the eighteenth-century developments on the land? Morineau dismisses many of these as ambiguous, 'the progress of misery'. In poor areas, such as Brittany and Lorraine, the introduction of the potato merely allowed a larger population to stay alive with a lower standard of living. No less importantly, Toutain appears to have burnt his fingers handling eighteenth-century statistical sources, causing him to exaggerate wildly the growth of agricultural output. A more realistic figure, proposed by Le Roy Ladurie, would be an increase in the range of 25 to 40 per cent between the 1700s and the 1780s.

This brings us to the other extreme in the debate, with those economists and historians who relegate agriculture to a 'weak' as opposed to a 'strong' role in overall development. To quote Boserup, 'it is reasonable to presume that as the general rule agriculture will exhibit a low supply elasticity which tends to act as a brake on economic growth'.[8] An agricultural system that was still 'stagnant, backward and primitive' in the mid-nineteenth century is an obvious candidate for explaining the alleged 'retardation' in French economic development. Paul Hohenberg, for example, has been influential in arguing that rural France was 'the seat of mechanisms working to offset, limit and tame the impulses for change that accompanied European modernization in the nineteenth century' [52]. Most of the blame for resistance to change in the countryside is laid at the door of the small peasant farmers, so characteristic of the tenurial system in France. The Revolutionary land settlement of the 1790s stands out in this perspective as an unfortunate turning point. Under pressure from a restive peasantry, the régime was compelled to confirm the existing subdivision of property and farms in many regions, and to accept the partial survival of collective rights. The stability (or more likely, the growth) of the peasantry during the nineteenth century can be gauged from official statistics of the 1880s on land ownership and farm size. To take one example, farms of less than 20 hectares (approximately 50 acres) covered two fifths of the surface area in France, compared to one fifth in Britain at the same period. Small farms, according to Tom Kemp, were 'bound to lack capital, technical knowledge and incentive or desire to break away from the traditional practices of husbandry' [58, *338*]. It follows that production for subsistence or for local markets loomed large in nineteenth-century French agriculture. Also, surplus labour was held on the land, creating labour shortages in industry.

Not all historians would agree with this common assumption that French agriculture in general, and its substantial peasant sector in particular, were the villains of the piece. An alternative case has slowly emerged among revisionist historians. To begin with, inevitably, it reassesses the timing of the transformation of agriculture. Evidence for an increase in crop yields under the *ancien régime* remains uncertain, but a study of yields for seven major cereal crops and potatoes points to a rapid increase over the period 1815–24 to 1865–74 (with a compound growth rate of 1.1 per cent a year). The source used here is not without problems: the best that can be said is that it produces a result close to the growth rate of 1.2 per cent a year calculated by Toutain for total agricultural output over the same period [85]. There is also the

Table 5.1 *Annual rates of growth of agricultural productivity (based on annual averages)*

	1830–1880	1880–1910
France	1.1	0.9
Germany	1.5	2.2
Belgium	1.1	1.4
Italy	0.2	0.8
Netherlands	0.4	1.5
United Kingdom	0.7	0.8
Russia	0.1	0.7
Switzerland	1.0	0.9
Europe	0.6	0.8

Source: P. Bairoch, 'Dix-huit décennies de développement agricole français dans une perspective internationale (1800–1980)', *Economie rurale*, 184–6 (1988), p. 21.

possibility that contemporaries and historians alike have neglected significant improvements in livestock rearing between 1750 and 1850, by focusing too narrowly on cereals [84]. Such changes were confined to a small number of regions to begin with, notably the Paris basin, with its large-scale capitalist farmers, its access to urban markets and its close contacts with England and the Netherlands. By contrast, much of the West, the South-West, the Centre and the mountain regions remained largely tied to the old system of polyculture, with few links to the market, until the latter part of the nineteenth century [34]. Even within a single department, the Pas-de-Calais, Hubscher notes a range of local variations at mid century, from the rich and intensive farming of Artois and the Béthunois to the backward Montreuillois, Boulonnais and Haut-Pays [54, I, *41–2*]. Taking the aggregate, Table 5.1 shows that the rate of growth of productivity in French agriculture was comfortably above the European average between 1830 and 1880. (The period after 1880 was another matter: the modest increase in productivity suggests that France, like Britain, may have missed out on an early 'green revolution' in European agriculture [105].)

In sum, it now starts to look as though the first stirrings of change in agriculture largely coincided with those in industry. Once this point is conceded, the argument that agricultural supply was a critical bottleneck during the early stages of industrialization becomes difficult to sustain. A more likely pattern was of a relatively elastic long-run agricultural supply during the late eighteenth and nineteenth centuries. Evidence of an agricultural revolution appearing as a 'splattering of oil drops' around the cities suggests that, wherever they could, farmers grasped the opportunities provided by new outlets for their produce. A recent survey concludes that 'farmers responded to the market after 1750 by working harder, investing more, and by shifting the balance of their crop mix towards more marketable productions' [44, *44*]. By 1870, France can be included in a select group of European countries with highly productive agriculture (although it has to be admitted that she came in some distance behind the others: Denmark, Britain, the Netherlands and Belgium) [105, *219*].

The revisionist case can also present small-scale farming in a more favourable light, once it is accepted that the backwardness of French agriculture may have been overdrawn. We might note a recent (though controversial) thesis within Marxist historiography, which completely reverses the conventional understanding of the Revolutionary land settlement. The assumption that agrarian capitalism could only develop with large-scale farming, on the English and physiocratic models is rejected out of hand. In the French case, with big landowners acting merely as *rentiers*, the 'most expansive and most democratic way to capitalist development' lay with small independent producers. Hence any 'negative aspects' of capitalist evolution in nineteenth-century France stemmed less from what the small peasants were able to impose on the bourgeois revolution (the persistence of the rural community), and more from what they failed to snatch from it (the destruction of large-scale property and the disappearance of landed rents) [80]. The thesis ends up appealing more to democratic principles than to economic efficiency; but it is worth remembering that development economists consider the redistribution of land as a possible route to increased productivity as well as to greater equality. It can hardly be a coincidence that small farms predominated in many of the more dynamic economies of

Europe, notably Belgium, Switzerland and Western Germany. For example, small peasant farms of 5 to 20 hectares in size accounted for 33.4 per cent of agricultural land in the western provinces of Germany in 1907 (compared to 24.8 per cent in France in 1882).[9]

More direct evidence from the early twentieth century can be adduced to show the potential dynamism of small farms in France. An official enquiry of 1909 pointed to better results on the small farms than on the large ones in a majority of departments, particularly those in southern France [55]. The report from the Allier was unequivocal:

> The small farmers have managed to profit from the general progress in methods of cultivation, the use of chemical fertilisers, the spread of selected seeds and the progress of livestock. The big landowners generally show no interest in farming. They lease their land to 'general farmers', who exploit it by means of sharecroppers.
>
> (From Ministère de l'Agriculture, *La Petite propriété rural en France*, 1909)

The possibility that results were biased by the prejudices of those conducting the enquiry cannot be ruled out. But it is more likely that in some regions, favourable soil conditions and improved outlets in nearby towns encouraged small farms to specialize for the market: 'peasants' became commercial farmers. Small-scale farming was particularly suited to livestock rearing, the production of fine wines, fruit growing and market gardening. Examples of successful adaptation to the market along these lines are legion: cattle raisers in Brittany, dairy farmers in the Pays d'Auge, vinegrowers in Burgundy, and market gardeners around Paris come to mind.

Finally, the revisionist interpretation draws attention to the limited opportunities for agricultural growth in the French economy. For example, its supporters willingly concede that the increase in production achieved during the nineteenth century was relatively modest by European standards. But they emphasize the influence of the peculiarly slow growth of population in France, which dampened the demand for foodstuffs. The following estimates comparing growth rates in France and Britain during the period 1820 to 1880 will illustrate the point:

	France	*Great Britain*
Population	0.3	1.3
Per capita product	1.2	1.2
Agricultural demand	0.9	1.9
Agricultural output	0.8	1.1

Such figures suggest that French farmers were just about able to provide an adequate supply of food [50]. Vernon Ruttan goes further, when looking at the period 1880 to 1930, claiming that 'the "inefficient" French peasant provided the urban-industrial sector with more food per capita and at lower real prices' [99]. Similarly, there is the argument that in so far as French peasants tended to stay on the land, it was because industry was slow to create new employment outlets for them. This was partly a matter of the gradual nature of French industrialization, partly a matter of a product mix which relied on an élite of skilled craftsmen rather than an army of unskilled labourers. 'As we learn more about the social history of French towns and the pace and pattern of internal migration in France', observe O'Brien and Keyder, 'it becomes harder to condemn people's decisions to remain where they were born as irrational'. The need to maintain a high density of labour in the countryside will in fact go a long way towards explaining the 'backwardness' of French agriculture. The pressure of numbers dictated an intensive cultivation of inferior soils and a crop mix dictated by basic cereals [91, *189–96*]. In short, there are now grounds for thinking that agriculture was neither a prime mover nor an obstacle during the development process. More in evidence was a certain 'balance' between the agricultural and industrial sectors during a long period of industrialization.

6
'The call of the markets': the pressure of demand in the French economy

An early symptom of change in the French economy during the eighteenth century was the increasingly hectic pace of activity in the great sea ports. The quaysides were laden with textiles, hardware, furniture, foodstuffs, wines, and brandies, destined for markets which doubtless sounded as exotic to contemporaries as they do to us: the Levant, Barbary, Oceania and the Antilles. A motley assortment of capitalists and sea-farers, spurred on by 'the taste for adventure, the spirit of enterprise and above all the search for profit', managed to establish France as one of the major trading nations of the world [15, II, *196*]. But the question remains as to how important these exports were in launching and sustaining the development of the economy. Could they be described as a 'leading sector', providing an external stimulus for the rest of the economy? Or is this to put the cart before the horse? In other words, were rising exports more a consequence than a cause of increased production? Needless to say, establishing a relationship between trade and development in a particular economy is never easy. As Kindleberger warns, the temptation for economic historians has been to assert that an expansion of exports promoted economic growth (or that a contraction slowed it), without specifying the mechanisms at work [60, *264*]. Of late, however, they have begun to take a more sophisticated approach, within the limitations of their sources. This can be seen in their coverage of two important issues: the influence of war and blockade between 1792 and 1815, and the extent of missed opportunities in the late nineteenth century.

To begin with, there is the proposition from Crouzet that 'the manifold and serious dislocations which international trade suffered during the Napoleonic Wars had an unfavourable and retardative effect upon the growth of Continental industry'. In the eighteenth century, he asserts, commercial expansion had been a 'strategic factor' in the growth of both British and French industry. But then the long period of war and blockade dealt the sea-borne trade of the 'Atlantic sector' in France a near-fatal blow. There was some compensation from the captive markets provided by Napoleon's Continental System, but on balance French industrial development was hindered more than the British by the disruption of trade. Indeed, the whole character of industrialization on the Continental mainland was allegedly transformed: economies that were outward-looking and geared for exports in the eighteenth century became introverted and orientated towards their home markets in the nineteenth [30, *17–20*, *32–7*, *295–317*; 9, *159–90*]. This very bald outline begs various questions, which have brought different answers from historians.

First, can one be more specific on the role played by exports in the development of French industry during the eighteenth century? The quantitative evidence gives some initial answers. Exports can be expressed as a percentage of national product as follows:

1720	8%
1750	12%
1780	10%

This ratio reveals a degree of openness to the world that was similar to that of the British economy. But it is clear that the potential stimulus to change was largely confined to the first half of the century [1, *57*]. Pierre Leon calculates that the value of exports increased by an average of 4.1 per cent a year between 1716 and 1748, compared to only 1 per cent and 1.4 per cent a year respectively during the periods 1749–78 and 1779–89. In other words, at a time when British foreign trade was steadily accelerating, France ran into the famous 'crisis of the Old Regime' during the late eighteenth century [15, II, *502–5*]. The structure of exports was also appropriate enough for a developing economy, with a little under half being manufactured goods (if colonial re-exports are left aside). But again, ominously, there was no sign of change in this proportion over the course of the century [1, *53–8*]. Some authorities have asserted that the impact of foreign trade was confined to a small, prosperous enclave, the 'maritime economy', which left the huge artisanal and peasant economy of 'la France profonde' undisturbed. This is probably an exaggeration. Demand from abroad was one factor encouraging industry to mobilize its part-time rural labour force, as well as its more skilled urban workers. The port of Rouen and Le Havre, for example, exported textile goods from a vast hinterland in northern and western France: 'cloths from Brittany, Combourg, Fougères, Morlaix, Mortagne and Vimoutiers; from Beauvais, Cholet, Laval, Rouen and Saint-Quentin; from Cambrai, Granada (*sic*) and Valenciennes' [31, *201*]. Yet there is no evidence to link the growth in exports with the introduction of new technologies into the manufacturing sector. And, as Asselain points out, the 'Atlantic sector' of the eighteenth century failed to produce any decisive changes in the future key industries of the Industrial Revolution [1, *69–70*].

This leads to a second question: how far did the short-term influence of war and blockade on external outlets merely accelerate underlying long-term changes in the economy? A number of studies have drawn attention to the cracks appearing in the huge edifice of maritime and colonial trade well before the 1790s. These included scores of complaints that French goods were being edged out of foreign markets by British competition. Thus cloth manufacturers from parts of Languedoc found themselves struggling in the Levant during the second half of the century. Similarly, merchants from Rouen and Bordeaux encountered cheaper products from Britain and America on their colonial markets in the West Indies [102, *5*; 32, *49*; 16, *254*]. A further sign of weakness was the failure of French producers to penetrate the North American market in the aftermath of the War of Independence. The United States was the most dynamic of the new, 'middle-class' markets appearing at the turn of the century. Yet, as Bergeron observes, even with peace-time conditions, the French would probably have lost out to their rivals [9, *478*]. Finally, one might wonder whether the collapse of so many industries in the West and South-West of France during the Revolutionary and Napoleonic eras was part of a long-term reorientation of the French economy. A promising regional development along the Atlantic coast, with American links akin to those of Lancashire perhaps, might have been snuffed out prematurely by the blockade. But it is also conceivable that industrial development was most likely to occur in the North and the East – part of what would later be known as the Golden Triangle of Western Europe [1, *69*; 36, *538–9*].

If some form of turning point in French trading patterns undoubtedly occurred between 1792 and 1815, another can also be discerned in the late nineteenth century. Until the 1870s, France was able to maintain her position as the second most important commercial power in the world, behind Britain. But by 1913 she had slipped to fourth place, having been usurped by Germany and the United States. In 1860, France accounted for an estimated 12.8 per cent of world exports; by 1913, her share had declined to 7.2 per cent [70, *38–9*]. Richard Roehl would presumably argue that such figures illustrate once again the originality of the French path to development. He suggests that most countries in Europe (including Germany, as a special case) were 'small-country' industrializers, whose growth was likely to be accelerated by export specialization. At the opposite pole, he awards France the designation of 'large' country, and contends that her export performance must be judged by different criteria [98, *458–63*]. Some support for this line comes from the statistics in Table 6.1 (though Bairoch warns readers not to place too much confidence in the figures he proposes!). Given that 'the importance of per capita foreign trade in the XIX century was in general in inverse proportion to the size of the country but in proportion to the level of development', it is not surprising that Switzerland, the UK and Belgium recorded high figures [3, *17*]. Conversely, Russia, Spain and Italy emerge predictably low in the classification, and France and Germany in the middle.

A number of studies also confirm that over most of the nineteenth century, exports were insufficiently dynamic to be an 'engine of growth' in France. During the first half of the century, French goods struggled with the crushing superiority established by the British overseas. In 1860, as in 1780, French commodity exports were only equivalent to 10.8 per cent of the national product, compared to a British figure of 15.3 per cent. And towards the end, they faced the debilitating effects of Depression and trade warfare. The third quarter of the century may have been an interlude of export-led growth. Between 1860 and 1880 the

Table 6.1 *Per capita exports of individual European countries, 1830–1910 (current dollars; three year annual averages)*

	1830(a)	1860	1880	1910
Austria-Hungary	1	4	8	9
Belgium	5	19	43	85
Denmark	6	12	20	45
France	3	11	15	29
Germany	3	11	16	27
Italy	2	4	7	11
Russia	1	2	3	5
Spain	1	3	7	9
Switzerland	12	31	50	60
United Kingdom	8	22	30	48
Europe	3	—	12	18

(a) The data are approximate for most of the countries.
Source: 'European Foreign Trade in the XIX Century: The Development of the Value and Volume of Exports (Preliminary Results)', *Journal of European Economic History*, 2 (1973).

economy grew at 1.1 per cent a year, while exports surged ahead at 2.35 per cent. France was at last able to take advantage of her favourable location in Western Europe, her investments abroad and the rising standard of living on the Continent [77, *LX–LXII*; 15, III, *336*; 73, *47–9*]. Jeanneney, however, concludes that this intensification of foreign trade was more a consequence than a cause of growth. He points to the appearance of a trade deficit after 1866, and the declining share of manufactured goods in the total of exports [56]. A similar dispute arises over the period 1896 to 1913. The majority of historians conclude that exports acted as a leading sector during these years of vigorous growth. From 15.0 per cent of GNP in 1887–96, exports increased to 17.1 per cent in 1907–13, allegedly giving a stimulus to the introduction of new technologies in the electrical, chemical and automobile industries [56, *52–3*; 73, *48*]. In this case it is Toutain who dissents, arguing that exports were dependent on the productive capacity of the economy [70, *63*].

Unlike Roehl, however, most historians consider that the relative decline of French exports on the international market from the 1880s reflected (and doubtless reinforced) some deep-seated weaknesses in the economy. They tend to dismiss any suggestion from contemporaries that France was large enough to be self-sufficient as a symptom of complacency. Hence there is little sympathy for the oft-quoted remark from Adolphe Thiers that 'We should avoid foreign competition, because we make everything' [15, III, *306*, IV, *199–200*]. They draw attention to deficiencies in the facilities for foreign trade: the ports, the merchant marine and the banking system. Most importantly of all, they emphasize the long-term stability in trading partners and commodities exported, which they feel inappropriate for a developing country. There is the remarkable finding that the proportion of manufactured goods in the total of French exports actually declined over the course of the century: from 73.9 per cent in 1837–1846 to 58.1 per cent in 1907–1913! And some of the areas where France had a 'revealed comparative advantage' at the turn of the century, notably alcohol and tobacco, clothing, and fancy goods (the famous *articles de Paris*), harked back to the luxury trades of the *ancien régime* [27]. With the benefit of hindsight, it is not difficult to see that French exports were heavily committed to industries that were destined to grow slowly in the twentieth century (textiles and clothing), but were weak in some of the more dynamic ones (metals, engineering, and chemicals). Table 6.2 shows how France fared in comparison with some of her rivals in this respect. The poor showing in the exports of machinery is often highlighted as a serious shortcoming in the modern world, as is a more general failure to export cheap, mass-produced goods. Not all was gloom at this period, however. On the eve of the First World War, France was the biggest exporter of cars in the world. She also managed to catch up with Britain and Germany in her export ratio (15.3 of GNP in 1910, compared to 17.5 per cent and 14.6 per cent respectively).

What emerges, then, is the paradox of exports whose volume increased prodigiously in the eighteenth and nineteenth centuries, but whose impact on the development of the economy was limited. It goes without saying that French prosperity was always to a considerable extent dependent on the external market. A simulation exercise suggested that a 1 per cent drop in the growth rate in foreign demand would have produced an overall drop of 7.2 per cent in GDP at the end of the period 1825–59 [73, *232*]. But there is no suggestion of the dazzling export-led growth that

Table 6.2 *Exports of manufactures in 1913 (percentages, based on values at current prices)*

	France	Belgium & Luxemburg	Germany	Italy	Switzerland	UK
Chemicals	10.0	14.3	13.8	7.0	6.9	6.1
Metals and metal goods	10.7	31.0	23.1	2.3	4.4	18.6
Machinery	3.6	4.6	13.4	2.8	10.3	9.7
Road vehicles and transport	6.7	7.7	3.8	3.8	1.5	6.4
Other manufactures	27.1	18.6	27.1	23.5	24.5	10.8
Textiles and clothing	41.9	23.8	18.8	60.6	52.4	48.4
Total	100.0	100.0	100.0	100.0	100.0	100.0

Source: A. Maizels, *Industrial Growth and World Trade* (Cambridge, 1963), Appendix A.

characterized British and German industrialization. This may well reflect a certain reluctance to venture abroad on the part of French businessmen, and a hesitancy to embrace new technologies. But Roehl is surely right to warn of the dangers of an anglocentric approach. France did after all enjoy some success in exploiting her own areas of comparative advantage, selling luxury products to the wealthier members of European society. One might therefore follow him in concluding that she came to settle into an intermediary position between 'small' countries like Britain and large, continental ones like the United States.

The corollary is that home demand loomed large in French economic development during the eighteenth and nineteenth centuries. According to one influential estimate, the national market accounted for between 75 and 80 per cent of all commercial transactions under the *ancien régime* [15, II, *180*]. The role of this type of demand in the French case has not aroused any notable controversies among historians. They generally acknowledge the advantages of having a relatively large population (an estimated 28.6 million in 1790), and of the extensive investments made in the economic infrastructure during the mid-nineteenth century. At the same time, they emphasize the various obstacles to the emergence of a demand for cheap, mass-produced goods. These include a peasantry that was in many cases too impoverished to buy manufactured goods on the market; wide disparities in income levels; a series of isolated, local markets (partly attributable to the size of the country, partly to a slow start in railway construction); and a preference among the bourgeoisie for high quality products [30, *32–7*; 91, *160–8*]. Transport improvements and new retailing methods gave boost to the national market from the 1830s onwards [15, III, *241–304*; 94]. Nonetheless, Lévy-Leboyer and Bourguignon contend that in the middle of the nineteenth century, during a phase of active industrialization, entrepreneurs 'lacked a large domestic consumption market which would have enabled them to realize the potential that technology, manpower and the nation's resources were then offering'. Even in the early twentieth century, this 'real deficiency in demand' was still apparent, with peasants devoting 76 per cent of their budgets to food, and urban working-class households 70 per cent [73, *27–46*]. This of course will help to explain why 'flexible specialization', as opposed to mass production, was so well suited to French conditions.

Overall, the pressure of demand in the French economy was generally muted before 1914. Marczewski has confronted a very rough estimate of aggregate demand for industrial goods (comprising agricultural purchasing power, state expenditure and the foreign trade balance) with industrial output in the nineteenth century. He concludes that there was only one period when demand ran ahead of supply, and that was in the exceptional circumstances of the Napoleonic Wars. During three others, the decades 1845–54, 1855–64 and 1905–13, the increase in demand was approximately equal to the increase in industrial production. During the first two of these, a considerable surge in all of the various components of demand was apparently met without difficulty by industry, since industrial prices remained stable. In the early twentieth century, by contrast, industrial prices rose sharply, but this Marczewski attributes to rising costs of production (rather than to excess demand), since agricultural prices rose even faster at the same period. Otherwise in the nineteenth century, between 1815–24 and 1845–54, and again between 1865–74 and 1895–

1904, demand lagged behind industrial output [77, *LXXI–LXXVII*]. Constraints on the demand side of the French economy will therefore go some way to explain the nature of French economic development [23, *215*]. In particular, on foreign markets French manufacturers soon found themselves squeezed into a small niche, between the well-established and highly-mechanized British, and newer rivals like the Swiss and Germans who had the potential advantage of very low wages. They were relatively secure on the international market for high quality goods, but this type of product was always vulnerable to a recession, and the scope for expansion was limited. Similarly, at home, despite formidable tariff and other barriers to imports, the narrowness and inelasticity of the market was a frequent lament from industrialists. Yet the fact remains that one of the functions of entrepreneurs is to create new markets. And in the last analysis, what is important for development is the response of the economy to a whole range of possible stimuli on both the supply and the demand sides [60, *287*; 104, *162–3*; 82].

7
Social and institutional influences on development

Economic historians, following in the footsteps of orthodox economists, have a tendency to explain the performance of an economy in material terms. As we have seen in earlier sections of the present work, differences in the level of development between countries can be attributed to differences in factor endowments, which can in turn be traced back to such influences as differences over time in, say, rates of population increase or saving. But we have also mentioned the statistical evidence which will show that increases in output can only partly be accounted for by increases in the physical inputs of land, labour and capital. Once again, the large 'residual' hovers over our search for explanations. And as soon as we start to consider the quality of labour or the efficient allocation of resources, a personal or 'human factor' comes into play. To be more precise, there is the possibility that the entrepreneurial abilities of a population can be an influence on development. At this point, economists and historians alike face an intractable problem. Can one assume that where economic conditions are ripe for development, entrepreneurs (defined by Casson as those who specialize in taking judgemental decisions about the coordination of scarce resources) will always appear, given the basic human motivation to maximize one's gains? Or should one go to the other extreme, and argue that entrepreneurs shape rather than are shaped by their circumstances, with the result that the success or failure of an economy can largely be attributed to the quality of its business leadership? In the first case, development can be entirely explained by conventional 'economic' considerations, and entrepreneurship is reduced to the status of a dependant variable. But in the second case, 'noneconomic' social and psychological influences come to the fore, and entrepreneurship must be deemed an independent variable.[10]

The heyday of the social type of interpretation in French economic history was the immediate post-Second World War period. This was when 'culture men' like David Landes [63] and John Sawyer [100] battled it out with 'coal men' like Rondo Cameron. Since then it has lost ground in the literature, not least because the whole drift of its argument was that the French pattern of 'retarded economic growth and industrialization' could be explained by the deficiencies of entrepreneurs [53]. Once a more favourable view of economic growth in France came into fashion, the ground was cut from under its feet [69]. Historians have found various material advantages in France, but nobody has yet been prepared to assert that exceptionally vigorous entrepreneurship emerged to promote growth. This has not prevented various authors continuing the tradition of the so-called 'Harvard School'. Thompson, for example, attributed the decline of the cloth-making industry in Clermont-de-Lodève during the second half of the eighteenth century to a combination of clumsy administrative intervention and 'entrepreneurial weakness' [102]. Trebilcock used a more general survey to mount a spirited counter-attack on the revisionist position, concluding that the time has come to resurrect the hypothesis of entrepreneurial deficiency [104]. And Reddy has recently observed in his study of the textile trades that 'economic conditions cannot be understood in isolation from the cultural and political dimensions that played as lively a role in shaping them as did the wider world commercial system' [95, *17*]. Although not particularly concerned with explaining French economic development, he does emphasize the slow emergence of an entrepreneurial class, and the obstacles this posed to the spread of new technology. The influence of Landes and his colleagues also persists insofar as they set the agenda for subsequent generations of historians. They have provoked discussion on a number of key issues, ranging from firm size to the role of government in business.

The Harvard School appears to have been moved by the supreme self-confidence of American capitalism during the 1940s and 1950s. The French entrepreneur was set beside a vision of modern corporate management – and cruelly exposed. Where the typical American business leader was thought to be innovative and forward looking, his French counterpart was allegedly conservative, cautious and of limited horizons. What were the reasons for this contrast? In the first place, American business was dominated by large, impersonal corporations, whereas in France most firms retained a family structure, characteristic of precapitalist economies. In the French system, according to Landes, 'the compulsive urge toward growth inherent in business for the sake of business is either diluted or absent' [63, *338*]. In the second place, America was a young country, where business could flourish in a bracing new social environment, whereas France bore the weight of traditional social relations and aristocratic values which 'tended to be contemptuous of the kind of aggressive commercial behaviour functionally inherent to an expanding capitalism' [100, *11*]. This heritage allegedly had an adverse effect on the recruitment, motivation and commercial behaviour of French entrepreneurs. But for opponents of this school among historians, such criticisms are all too obviously based on the American experience, failing to take sufficient account of the conditions in which the French *patronat* had to operate.

First, then, the recruitment of 'strong wills and strong intellects' into business may have been impeded by the higher status attached to administrative careers, and the temptation for successful entrepreneurs or their sons to ape the lifestyle of the nobility on a landed estate [100, *14–15*]. One could argue that there was a 'dearth of heroes' in the late eighteenth and early nineteenth centuries, creating an 'efficiency gap' which had to be filled by foreign entrepreneurs: the likes of Holker, Oberkampf, Wilkinson and Alcock. One could also cite the case of the bourgeoisie in Normandy, who revealed an almost indecent haste to put their money into land. Most spectacular was the cotton spinner Pouyer-Quertier, who rose from a relatively modest background to establish the massive La Foudre mill in 1860, but who frittered most of his fortune marrying off his two daughters to a count and a marquis. Yet, as Jean-Pierre Chaline points out, cotton manufacture in Normandy was an exceptionally risky business, since specialization in the cheaper range of goods meant that the region had to bear the brunt of British competition. 'A certain lucidity' may therefore be detected in the speculative approach to industry so characteristic of Norman entrepreneurs [22, *108–16*, *372–7*; 72, *43–56*]. There was indeed a regional dimension to entrepreneurial strategies. If the Normans (in cotton spinning especially) had a tendency to withdraw from industry as soon as possible, industrialists in Flanders and above all in Alsace established some impressive dynasties. A recent study has shown that in 1885 no less than four-fifths of large firms in Alsace were run by the third, fourth or even fifth generation of a family: the famous Schlumbergers, Dollfus, Miegs, Koechlins and so on [72, *9–25*].

The motivation of French entrepreneurs can also be called into question. Was it a matter of employers sacrificing the growth of their firms in the interests of family security, as Landes would argue? Or was it more a matter of small firms sacrificing family profits and security to growth, as Lévy-Leboyer suggests? [69, *7*]. A reluctance to innovate, or a preference for leisure over work, could always be attributed to the stifling influence of family firms and 'pre-industrial' values. But once again, there were the industrialists from Alsace, whose commitment to education, scientific research and patriarchal welfare schemes, as well as to the aggrandizement of their family firms, has become almost legendary. Michel Hau in fact considers family solidarity to have been one of the great strengths of the Alsatian *patronat* [49]. The mill owners of the Nord, and the ironmasters of Lorraine, emerge as other examples of groups who were no less solid in their family ties, and no less relentless in their application to industrial affairs. The suspicion must be that French entrepreneurs, no less than their rivals abroad, lived and breathed business [66, II, *155-6*; 8].

Their behaviour in the market brings a further test. For their critics, the relatively small size of French firms compared to the competition in Europe and North America, and the reluctance of large firms to gobble up the minnows around them, is a major sign of entrepreneurial weakness. Alternatively, it may be that the disadvantages of large firms under prevailing conditions in nineteenth-century France, and the corresponding advantages of small ones, have been overlooked [41]. Around 1830, textile manufacturers in Alsace became aware of the vulnerability of huge conglomerates to a recession, and so divided firms according to their specialization in spinning, weaving and printing. Similarly, from the 1880s onwards, cotton manufacturers in Normandy learned the hard way that modest-sized family firms were better able to ride the storms of the business cycle than large corporations [67, *474*; 22, *153–4*]. The small firm, as we have already noted, was arguably well suited to French conditions, given the potential for 'flexible specialization' rather than for standardization and mass production. In particular, it may be seen as appropriate to the decentralization of many French markets, and the strength of demand for high quality goods – as Landes himself recognized [63, *340–6*]. The small firm also provided a favourable environment for motivating the skilled labour on which industry relied so heavily [69]. Interestingly, a study of firm size in textiles and flour milling during the 1860s concludes that 'By any standard the estimates of returns to scale are rather low, and most firms would not have stood to gain much in efficiency simply by being larger' [89, *648*]. In sum, French industry undoubtedly had a 'dualistic' structure, in the sense that a substantial body of small enterprises persisted beside a kernel of very large firms. But some degree of this type of dualism can be found in all industrial societies. And if in the French case some preference for small-scale, high-quality production can partly be attributed to social and cultural influences, more significant (in our view) is the evidence to show entrepreneurs reacting rationally to their economic environment [69; 71].

One final, and very important, aspect of entrepreneurship which remains to be discussed concerns the role of government. A frequent accusation is that French business leaders allowed themselves to become dependent on various forms of state support, preferring a steady but secure existence to the risky but ultimately more profitable strategy of going for growth on the open market. Bert Hoselitz asserted that the willingness of governments under the *ancien régime* and the First Empire to bail out enterprises making losses or to subsidize others which could never have survived on their own undermined the 'spirit of venturesomeness' in France [53].

One could always go to the opposite extreme, and argue that the state did not do enough to help businessmen compete on world markets. A case could be made that to overcome various obstacles, French entrepreneurs needed more rather than less in the way of technical assistance, vocational training schemes and protection of trade routes. How effective, then, was the French state in clearing away institutional obstacles to enterprise, and in using its resources to stimulate business activity?

To begin with, we must look back briefly to the 'mercantilist' policies of the seventeenth and eighteenth centuries, associated in France with the name of Jean-Baptiste Colbert. These set out to encourage industry and commerce by state intervention on two fronts: on the one hand, with a very tight system of regulation to maintain high standards, and on the other, with a series of subsidies, loans and privileges to support individual entrepreneurs [35]. The strategy was arguably appropriate enough for the conditions of early modern Europe, with a relatively static market for a few high-quality products. But by the 1750s it was beginning to look jaded. There was the risk of corruption, as success came to depend more on the diplomatic skills required for the manipulation of officials than on business acumen. There was also the growing market for lower quality goods, which outflanked the regulated sector [102, *457–8*]. The ground was thus prepared for the gradual shift to a more liberal régime in the economy which occurred during the second half of the eighteenth century. Evidence can certainly be found to show businessmen struggling to come to terms with freer markets. As we have already noted, Thomson attributes the decline of the woollen industry in Clermont-de-Lodève to entrepreneurial weakness, or to be more specific, to a mass exodus from the business of a generation of entrepreneurs who had over-expanded under the cover of the old system, and who then declined to compete in the new one [102]. Over the same period, merchants in the fine linen trade of Valenciennes experienced similar withdrawal symptoms when confronted with liberalization. As late as 1822, twelve of them set up an agency to supervise the quality of their batistes, attempting (illegally as it turned out) to persist with the traditional approach of wooing an élite clientèle with a seal of official approval on their products [45, I, *96*]. Yet the scale of this type of commitment to the 'Colbert model' can be overdrawn. Perhaps most significantly, one can point to the fact that businessmen tended to support the Revolution, in its early, moderate phase, and its wholesale abolition of regulations and royal manufactures, not to mention of guilds, internal customs duties and all vestiges of the seigneurial system [11; 78, *698–706*]. The rather odd result was that the legislative framework for the capitalist system, based on private property rights and individual liberty, was in place in France well before industrial capitalism developed on any scale [1, *120*]. To pursue the point further, it might be suggested that any 'nannying' of businessmen with regulations was far outweighed by the inability of the French state to create some of the basic conditions for enterprise. Internally, public finances were a shambles during the *ancien régime* and Revolution; tolls and internal customs duties hampered the movement of goods before 1789; and political stability remained elusive throughout the nineteenth century. Externally, trading routes were always vulnerable to blockade by the British because of a neglect of naval power: as Crouzet notes, 'Britain's rise to economic ascendancy was accompanied by a succession of military and political successes, which made her first a great power, then the super-power; those successes were mainly achieved over France' [30, *3*]. The career of the merchant-iron-master Chaussade illustrates these points perfectly, as he wrestled under the *ancien régime* with a vexatious system of privilege, bureaucracy and dynastic warfare [7].

Bearing in mind these and other obstacles to development in France, efforts to manipulate taxes, subsidies and markets to promote private enterprise are more easily justified. Rather than an abuse of state patronage, they can be depicted as part of an effort to keep abreast of the front runners in the international economy. There were of course plenty of fiascos. Several of the Royal Manufactures launched in the eighteenth century were 'lame ducks' from day one, notable for their absurd pretensions and incompetent management. Take the *Manufacture royale de mousselines du Puy*, founded in 1755. It soon proved to be a misconceived attempt to develop industry in an unsuitable region, foundering when royal privileges were withdrawn [81, *128–31*]. And many of the subsidies granted by the Third Republic in the late nineteenth century served merely to shore up existing vested interests, such as sailing ships in the merchant marine or small retailers, rather than to promote innovations [62, *15–20*; 104, *184–6*]. More positively, though, after 1753 the system of privileged manufactures was wielded by Daniel Trudaine and his colleagues with clearly discernible priorities. New ventures in established luxury manufactures, such as lace and tapestries, were left entirely to private enterprise, whilst initiatives in various branches of French industry that were struggling to establish themselves, notably silk throwing, cotton spinning and metal-working, were consistently supported by the state [35, *627–9*]. At the same time, the state founded spinning schools, sent observers to Britain, imported foreign specialists and published technical works. Napoleon followed suit during the 1800s, driven, according to one of his ministers, by 'an aversion for the English and the desire to harm their industry'. Such measures had durable influence insofar as they helped the diffusion of mechanized methods in French industry, above all in cotton spinning [6, *10–14*, *30–6*; 10, *175–80*]. Later in the century, state intervention along these lines included subsidies to help French industry face the full force of British competition after the free-trade treaty of 1860; a series of universal exhibitions; and, after 1880, some tentative efforts to promote technical schools for workers. Finally, underpinning all of these initiatives, there was the policy of protecting the home market with tariffs and prohibitions.

Conventional wisdom would have it that while Britain boldly pioneered free trade policies in the middle of the nineteenth century, France remained firmly wedded to protectionism – until jolted by Napoleon III's economic *coup* of 1860. But Nye has recently asserted that this view is 'simply wrong'. He shows that French tariff rates were substantially below British rates between the 1820s and 1850s: the supposed period of 'high protection'. Thus in 1821–5 customs duties accounted for 53.1 per cent of import values in Britain, but only 20.3 per cent in France. By the late 1850s the disparity had narrowed, but the respective figures for Britain and France were still 15.0 and 10.0 per cent [89]. The significance of 1860 as a turning point can also be challenged. Messerlin notes that the overall level of protection in the French economy fell continuously from the 1840s to 1871. The 1860 treaty therefore emerges merely as confirmation of a policy of opening the French economy to the world which had already begun under the July Monarchy [64, *80*]. Nonetheless, French governments did make determined efforts to protect specific industries during the late eighteenth and early nineteenth centuries, and in France, unlike Britain, there was some resurgence of protectionism after 1871.

The heavy protectionism of the Revolutionary and Napoleonic régimes must be placed in the context of economic as well as military warfare with Britain [36; 10, *173*; 30, *295–317*]. For purist free-traders, the unfortunate by-products of this period were the creation of a series of 'hot-house' industries, which could not hope to survive on the market under normal conditions, and an addiction among entrepreneurs to tariffs and prohibitions. But one might counter with the 'infant-industry' argument. Assuming that France had the basic conditions for, say, mechanized cotton spinning, some respite from the full force of British competition could be beneficial during the early stages of its development. The protectionist stance of industrialists after 1815 might be deemed a rational response to persisting difficulties in establishing themselves on the international market. The record suggests that some of them at least were vigorously exploiting their areas of comparative advantage behind the trade barriers, seeking out new technologies, new products and new outlets, as in the case of calico-printers around Mulhouse and worsted manufacturers in Flanders [67; 78, *711–18*]. The main criticisms would then have to be that French entrepreneurs had some tendency to exaggerate the threat of foreign competition, and that the state might usefully have gone further in scaling down the level of protectionism (particularly on intermediate goods) during the 1820s and 1830s [51; 49, *234*].

The return to protectionism during the late nineteenth century was on a relatively modest scale, and in very different circumstances from the 1790s. The main influences were an economic crisis, affecting agriculture in particular, and a general raising of tariffs in neighbouring countries. Once again, there is a persuasive free-trade critique of such measures, emphasizing that they discouraged agriculture and industry from adapting their structures to changing world conditions. Secure behind its barriers, France at this period can be depicted as a 'stalemate society': one that would accept industrialization, but only on the basis of a compromise with the existing order.[11] Bairoch has countered that the usual association of protectionism with stagnation and free trade with growth cannot be sustained. He asserts that 'less developed' continental countries like France fared poorly compared to Britain during the period of free trade between 1860 and 1892. But during the period 1892 to 1914 the protected economies on the continent outstripped free-trade Britain, both in terms of increased foreign trade and more rapid economic growth [78, *36-90*]. Such conclusions, which appear on the surface to fly in the face of common sense, have not convinced everyone. Critics have pointed to the difficulties encountered when attempting to draw up clear-cut distinctions between 'free trade' and 'protectionist' periods, and the reluctance to explain how protectionism might stimulate the economy. The fact remains that the raising of tariffs from the 1880s was followed by a growing integration of the French economy into world markets, and dynamic entrepreneurial activity in certain industries, such as electro-chemicals, rubber, aluminium and motor cars [64; 1, *179–88*]. Furthermore, historians have recently noted that the capitalist interests which secured an alliance with small producers among the peasantry and petite bourgeoisie by means of the Meline tariff in 1892 were not necessarily refusing to adapt to a harsh reality. Rather they were seeking a framework of stability for their enterprises, in the face of threats from political extremists on both the left and the right.[12]

In conclusion, social and institutional influences on economic development can be used to explain a great deal – or very little. The underlying methodological problem here is always the one of finding yardsticks by which to judge the performance of entrepreneurs in particular. Inevitably historians must in the end rely on subjective assessments of qualitative evidence. Our inclination is to play down this type of influence. Certainly many of the criticisms of entrepreneurs and of government policy now appear overdrawn, bearing in mind the environment in which French industry had to operate and the desire to emulate foreign rivals. At the same time, to dismiss out of hand the socio-political context for industrialization would be unwise. Some rather odd paradoxes emerge in this sphere. We have businessmen showing some inclination to rely on a state which was itself notoriously unstable for much of our period. And we have the bizarre spectacle of an increasingly 'bourgeois' society whose role in the international market was to satisfy 'aristocratic' demand for a whole range of luxury products including perfumes, champagne, fine porcelain, high fashions and expensive motor cars [15, IV, *199–212*].

8
Conclusion

Asked at a televised press conference why he had risked alienating international opinion by selling gunboats to Israel, President Pompidou replied that the 'dear old France' of fine cuisine and the Folies-Bergère was finished. Contemporary France (of the early 1970s), he proudly asserted, had become a modern industrial nation, beholden to no one. The path to economic development was indeed a long one, and the links between profit and power were much in evidence all along. France must now be classed as one of the early starters among the industrializing nations. In the eighteenth century, administrators there grasped that her status as a great power would be put in jeopardy if she failed to emulate some of the innovations (notably in metallurgy) being pioneered by the British. As we have seen, she enjoyed some success in achieving this aim, even though developing in competition with such a formidable naval and economic power was bound to be an uphill struggle during the early stages. By the standards of the 1950s and 1960s at least, the economic growth of the eighteenth and nineteenth centuries may now appear relatively slow. And there is no disputing that many of the old structures in agriculture and industry survived through until the middle of the twentieth century. Nonetheless, this pattern of gradual development followed by rapid acceleration after the Second World War was common to all of the developing nations, even if the contrast between periods was more marked in France than in Britain and the United States.

For a full understanding of this development process in France, certain key questions need to be kept in mind. First, is it economic growth, industrialization or some more general notion of development that is being assessed? Secondly, what were the respective roles of internal and external factors, the latter of course subject to the impact of wars and blockades on international trade? Thirdly, and most importantly, did business leaders adapt successfully to factor prices and market opportunities, or did they sacrifice out-and-out growth to a slightly desperate bid for comfortable mediocrity? Students of the subject would also do well to put aside various 'anglo-saxon' prejudices, concerning 'inefficient' French peasants, for example, or, on the other side of the coin, 'Gallic flair' (which on the business side risked becoming an inflexible policy of high prices for high-quality goods). In the final analysis, though, should one conclude that the gradual path to development taken by the French was admirably humane? This is a point that would doubtless have been lost on, say, inhabitants of the slum quarters of Lille, or impoverished peasants in the Auvergne. The influence of protectionism and social conservatism was also more in evidence among the élite than any form of humanitarianism.

Yet the fact does remain that France managed to avoid the scale of distress evident among groups such as the British handloom weavers, not to mention the disastrous turn taken by German political life in the wake of rapid industrialization. Our inclination therefore is to stress the underlying shrewdness and economic rationality of the French population. They after all engineered a balance between agriculture and industry, and between higher incomes and social stability.

Notes

1 J.-J. Carré, P. Dubois and E. Malinvaud, *French Economic Growth* (London, 1976), pp. 165–6.
2 For interesting discussions of the regional dimension, see S. Pollard, *Peaceful Conquest: The Industrialization of Europe, 1760–1970* (Oxford, 1981); and P. K. O'Brien, 'Do We Have a Typology for the Study of European Industrialization in the XIXth Century?', *Journal of European Economic History* 15 (1986).
3 S. Kuznets, *Economic Growth of Nations* (Cambridge, Mass., 1971), Ch. II; M. Abramovitz, *Thinking about Growth* (Cambridge, 1989), pp. 3–79; N. F. R. Crafts, *British Economic Growth during the Industrial Revolution* (Oxford, 1985), pp. 70–88.
4 M. Abramovitz, 'Introduction' to National Bureau of Economic Research, *Capital Formation and Economic Growth* (Princeton, 1955), p. 4.
5 N. Rosenberg, *Inside the Black Box: Technology and Economics* (Cambridge, 1982), pp. 23–5.
6 C. F. Sabel, *Work and Politics* (Cambridge, 1982); M. J. Piore and C. F. Sabel, *The Second Industrial Divide* (New York, 1984); C. F. Sabel and J. Zeitlin, 'Historical Alternatives to Mass Production: Politics, Markets and Technology in Nineteenth-Century Industrialization', *Past and Present*, 108 (1985) 133–76.
7 Sabel, *Work and Politics*, p. 42.
8 M. Boserup, 'Agrarian Structure and Take-off', in W. W. Rostow (ed.), *The Economics of Take-off into Sustained Growth* (London, 1965).
9 See M. Tracy, *Government and Agriculture in Western Europe, 1880–1988* (Hemel Hempstead, 1989).
10 P. H. Wilken, *Entrepreneurship* (Norwood, N.J., 1979); and M. Casson, *The Entrepreneur* (Oxford, 1982).
11 S. Hoffmann, 'Paradoxes of the French Political Community', in Hoffmann and others (eds), *France: Change and Tradition* (London, 1963), pp. 3–5.

12 See M. S. Smith, *Tariff Reform in France*, 1860–1900 (Ithaca, N.Y., 1980); R. Magraw, *France, 1815–1914* (London, 1983), pp. 225–34; and H. Lebovics, *The Alliance of Iron and Wheat in the Third French Republic, 1860–1914* (Baton Rouge, 1988).

Select bibliography

Items marked with a star (*) contain extensive bibliographical references. Works are referred to in the text by number, followed by page reference in italics if necessary e.g. [1, *26*].

*[1] Asselain, J.-C., *Histoire économique de la France du XVIIIe siècle à nos jours*, Vol. 1 (Paris, 1984). The best succinct survey available; bibliography in second volume.

[2] Bairoch, P., 'Niveaux de développement économique de 1810 à 1910', *Annales ESC*, 20 (1965).

[3] —, 'European Foreign Trade in the XIX Century: The Development of the Value and Volume of Exports (Preliminary Results)', *Journal of European Economic History*, 2 (1973).

[4] —, 'Europe's Gross National Product: 1800–1975', *Journal of European Economic History*, 5 (1976).

[5] —, 'International Industrialization Levels from 1750 to 1980', *Journal of European Economic History*, 11 (1982).

[6] Ballot, C., *L'Introduction du machinisme dans l'industrie française* (Lille, 1923). A 'golden oldie': stands the test of time well.

[7] Bamford, P. W., *Privilege and Profit: A Business Family in Eighteenth-Century France* (Philadelphia, 1988).

[8] Barbier, F., *Le Patronat du Nord sous le Second Empire* (Geneva, 1989).

[9] Bergeron, L., 'Problèmes économiques de la France napoléonienne', *Revue d'histoire moderne et contemporaine*, 17 (1970).

[10] —, *France under Napoleon*, translated by R. R. Palmer (Princeton, N.J., 1981). Contains an excellent section on 'Economic Life'.

[11] Bonin, H., 'La Révolution française a-t-elle brisé l'esprit d'entreprise?', *L'Information historique*, 5 (1985).

[12] Bouvier, J. 'The Banking Mechanism in France in the Late 19th Century', in R. Cameron (ed.), *Essays in French Economic History* (Homewood, Ill., 1970). A useful introduction from the leading French authority in this area.

[13] —, 'Rapports entre systèmes bancaires et entreprises industrielles dans la croissance européenne au XIXe siècle', in CNRS, *L'Industrialisation en Europe au XIXe siècle* (Paris, 1972).

[14] Bouvier, J., 'Libres propos autour d'une démarche revisionniste', in P. Fridenson and A. Straus (eds), *Le Capitalisme français, 19e–20e siècle* (Paris, 1987). A stimulating essay reviewing recent debates in French economic history.

*[15] Braudel, F. and Labrousse, E., *Histoire économique et sociale de la France*, Vol. II (Paris, 1970); Vol. III (Paris, 1976); Vol. IV/1 (Paris, 1979). Remains the authoritative textbook in its field, though beginning to feel dated.

[16] Butel, P., *Les Négociants bordelais, l'Europe et les Îles au XVIIIe siècle* (Paris, 1974). An impressive study of a major Atlantic port.

[17] Cameron, R. E., 'Economic Growth and Stagnation in France, 1815–1914', *Journal of Modern History*, 30 (1958).

[18] —, *Banking in the Early Stages of Industrialization* (New York, 1967). Includes an influential chapter on France by Cameron.

*[19] Cameron, R. E., and Freedeman, C., 'French Economic Growth: A Radical Revision', *Social Science History*, 7 (1983). Lives up to its title: stands as the most radical of the 'revisionist' works.

[20] Caron, F., 'La Stratégie des investissements en France aux 19e et 20e siècles', *Revue d'histoire économique et sociale*, 54 (1976).

[21] Cayez, P., *Crises et croissance de l'industrie lyonnaise, 1850–1900* (Lyon, 1980). A good example of a local study in economic history.

[22] Chaline, J.-P., *Les Bourgeois de Rouen* (Paris, 1982). A superb monograph: massively researched but written with a certain lightness of touch.

[23] Chapman, S. D., and Chassagne, S., *European Textile Printers in the 18th Century: A Study of Peel and Oberkampf* (London, 1981). An interesting venture into comparative history, with useful material drawn from a more detailed study of Oberkampf (written in French) by Chassagne.

[24] Cipolla, C. M. (ed.), *The Fontana Economic History of Europe*, Vol. 3, (London, 1973). Controversial chapter by P. Bairoch on Agriculture.

[25] Clough, S. B., 'Retardative Factors in French Economic Development in the Nineteenth and Twentieth Centuries', *Journal of Economic History*, 6, Supplement (1946). One of the earliest 'anglo-saxon' contributions to the debate.

[26] Crafts, N. F. R., 'Economic Growth in France and Britain, 1830–1910: A Review of the Evidence', *Journal of Economic History*, 44 (1984). An early questioning of the 'revisionist' position in French economic history.

[27] —, 'Revealed Comparative Advantage in Manufacturing, 1899–1950', *Journal of European Economic History*, 18 (1989), 127–37.

[28] Cross, G., *Immigrant Workers in Industrial France* (Philadelphia, 1983).

[29] Crouzet, F., 'French Economic Growth in the Nineteenth Century Reconsidered', *History*, 59 (1974).

*[30] —, *Britain Ascendant: Comparative Studies in Franco-British Economic History* (Cambridge, 1990). A collection of essays by one of the leading figures in French (and British!) economic history.

[31] Dardel, P., *Navires et marchandises dans les ports de Rouen et du Havre au XVIIIe siècle* (Paris, 1963).

[32] —, *Commerce, industrie et navigation à Rouen et au Havre au XVIIIe siècle* (Rouen, 1966).

[33] Daviet, J-P., *Un Destin internationale: la Compagnie de Saint-Gobain de 1830 à 1939* (Paris, 1988). A well-documented and readable business history.

[34] Demonet, M., *Tableau de l'agriculture française au milieu du 19e siècle: l'enquête de 1852* (Paris, 1990).

[35] Deyon, P. and Guignet, P., 'The Royal Manufactures and Economic and Technological Progress in France before the Industrial Revolution', *Journal of European Economic History*, 9 (1980). A preliminary synthesis of the literature.

[36] Dufraisse, R., 'Régime douanier, blocus, système continental', *Revue d'histoire économique et sociale* (1966).

*[37] Dupaquier, J. and others, *Histoire de la population française*, vol. II, *De la Renaissance à 1789* (Paris, 1988).

[38] Fremdling, R., 'Foreign Trade Patterns, Technical Change, Cost and Productivity in the West European Iron Industries, 1820–1870', in R. Fremdling and P. K. O'Brien (eds), *Productivity in the Economies of Europe* (Stuttgart, 1982).

[39] Fridenson, P., 'Une industrie nouvelle: l'automobile en France jusqu'en 1914', *Revue d'histoire moderne et contemporaine*, 19 (1972).

[40] —, 'France-Etats-Unis: Genèse de l'usine nouvelle', *Recherches*, 32–3 (1978).

[41] Gaillard, J., 'La Petite entreprise en France au XIXe et XXe siècle', in Commission internationale d'histoire des mouvements sociaux et des structures sociales, *Petite industrie et croissance industrielle dans le monde aux XIXe et XXe siècles* (2 vols, Paris, 1981).

[42] Geiger, R., *The Anzin Coal Company, 1800–1833* (Newark, Del., 1974).

[43] Gillet, M., *Les Charbonnages du Nord de la France au XIXe siècle* (Paris, 1973).

[44] Grantham, G., 'Agricultural Supply during the Industrial Revolution: French Evidence and European Implications', *Journal of Economic History*, 49 (1989).

[45] Guignet, P., *Mines, manufactures et ouvriers du Valenciennois au XVIIIe siècle* (2 vols, New York, 1977).

[46] Gullickson, G. L., *Spinners and Weavers of Auffay* (Cambridge, 1986). Contains abundant material on 'proto-industrialization'.

[47] Harris, J. R., *Industry and Technology in the Eighteenth Century: Britain and France* (Birmingham, 1972). An excellent 'grass-roots' view of this subject.

[48] —, 'The Diffusion of English Metallurgical Methods to Eighteenth-Century France', *French History*, 2 (1988).

[49] Hau, M., *L'Industrialisation de l'Alsace* (Strasbourg, 1987).

*[50] Heywood, C., 'The Role of the Peasantry in French Industrialization, 1815–80', *Economic History Review*, 2nd series, 34 (1981a).

[51] —, 'The Launching of an "Infant Industry"? The Cotton Industry of Troyes under Protectionism, 1793–1860', *Journal of European Economic History*, 10 (1981b).

[52] Hohenberg, P., 'Change in Rural France in the Period of Industrialization, 1830–1914', *Journal of Economic History*, 32 (1972).

[53] Hoselitz, B. F., 'Entrepreneurship and Capital Formation in France and Britain since 1700', in National Bureau of Economic Research, *Capital Formation and Economic Growth* (Princeton, N.J., 1955).

[54] Hubscher, R., *L'Agriculture et la société rurale dans le Pas-de-Calais du milieu du XIXe siècle à 1914* (2 vols, Arras, 1979). A recent example of the massive local studies produced by French historians.

[55] —, 'La Petite exploitation en France: réproduction et competivité (fin XIXe siècle–début XXe siècle)', *Annales ESC*, 40 (1985). Investigates the way small peasant farmers operated.

[56] Jeanneney, J.-M., 'Relations historiques entre l'intensité des commerces extérieurs et la croissance des produits nationaux', *Observations et diagnostics économiques*, 3 (1983), 51–63.

[57] Katznelson, I. and Zolberg, A. R. (eds), *Working-Class Formation* (Princeton, 1986). See chapters on French labour by A. Cottereau and M. Perrot.

[58] Kemp, T., 'Structural Factors in the Retardation of French Economic Growth', *Kyklos*, 15 (1962). An influential exposition of the retardation thesis.

[59] —, 'French Economic Performance: Some New Views Critically Examined', *European History Quarterly*, 15 (1985). A critique of 'revisionist' works by Roehl (1976), O'Brien and Keyder (1978) and Heywood (1981a).

[60] Kindleberger, C. P., *Economic Growth in France and Britain, 1851–1950* (Cambridge, Mass., 1964). Still worth reading for its lucid exposition of economic theory and economic history.

*[61] —, *A Financial History of Western Europe* (London, 1984).
[62] Kuisel, R. F., *Capitalism and the State in Modern France* (Cambridge, 1981). First chapter outlines 'The Liberal Order of 1900'.
[63] Landes, D., 'French Business and the Businessman: A Social and Cultural Analysis', in E. M. Earle (ed.), *Modern France* (Princeton, N.J., 1951). Classic statement of the 'socio-cultural' explanation of French economic development.
[64] Lassudrie-Duchêne, B. and Reiffers, J.-L. (eds), *Le Protectionnisme* (Paris, 1985). Includes useful articles on the nineteenth century by J.-C. Asselain, B. Desaigues and P. Messerlin.
[65] Lequin, Y., *Les Ouvriers de la région lyonnaise* (1848–1914) (2 vols, Lyon, 1977). One of the best regional studies to appear in the last few years.
*[66] — (ed), *Histoire des français XIXe–XXe siècles* (3 vols, Paris, 1983–4). Fine surveys of the British view of the French by C. Lucas, of rural society by R. Hubscher and of business leadership by L. Bergeron.
[67] Lévy-Leboyer, M., *Les Banques européennes et l'industrialisation internationale dans la première moitié du XIXe siècle* (Paris, 1964). A mine of information and ideas.
[68] —, 'Les Processus d'industrialisation: le cas de l'Angleterre et de la France', *Revue historique*, 239 (1968).
[69] —, 'Le Patronat français a-t-il été malthusien?', *Le Mouvement social* (1974).
[70] — (ed.), *La Position internationale de la France* (Paris, 1977).
[71] —, 'The Large Corporation in Modern France', in A. D. Chandler and H. Daems, *Managerial Hierarchies* (Cambridge, Mass., 1980).
[72] — (ed.), Special issue of *Le Mouvement social*, 132 (1985), entitled 'Dynasties patronales françaises', which includes essays on Alsace by M. Hau and Normandy by J.-P. Chaline.
[73] Lévy-Leboyer M., and Bourguignon, F., *The French Economy in the Nineteenth Century: An Essay in Econometric Analysis* (Cambridge, 1990). An influential work, though far from 'user-friendly'.
[74] Locke, R. R., 'French Industrialization: The Roehl Thesis Reconsidered', *Explorations in Economic History*, 18 (1981).
[75] Maddison, A., *Phases of Capitalist Development* (Oxford, 1982).
[76] Marczewski, J., 'The Take-Off Hypothesis and French Experience', in W. W. Rostow (ed.), *The Economics of Take-off into Sustained Growth* (London, 1963).
[77] —, 'Le Produit physique de l'économie française de 1789 à 1913 (comparaison avec la Grande Bretagne)', *Cahiers de l'ISEA* (Paris, 1965). A major (and much cited) source of data.
*[78] Mathias, P. and Pollard, S. (eds), *The Cambridge Economic History of Europe*, vol. VIII, *The Industrial Economies: The Development of Economic and Social Policies* (Cambridge, 1989). Comprehensive

chapters on European Trade Policy by P. Bairoch and French Economic and Social Policies by T. Kemp.

*[79] Mathias, and Postan, M. (eds), *The Cambridge Economic History of Europe*, vol. VII, *The Industrial Economies: Capital, Labour and Enterprise*, part 1, (Cambridge, 1978). Useful chapters on Entrepreneurship and Management by C. Fohlen and Capital Formation by M. Lévy-Leboyer.

*[80] McPhee, P., 'A Reconsideration of the "Peasantry" of Nineteenth-Century France', *Peasant Studies*, 9 (1981).

[81] Merley, J., *La Haute-Loire de la fin de l'ancien régime aux débuts de la Troisième République* (Le Puy, 1974).

[82] Mill, A. W., 'French Steel and the Metal-Working Industries: A Contribution to Debate on Economic Development in Nineteenth-Century France', *Social Science History*, 9 (1985).

[83] Morineau, M., *Les Faux-semblants d'un démarrage économique: agriculture et démographie en France au XVIIIe siècle* (Paris, 1971). Presents a dismal view of French agriculture.

[84] Mulliez, J., 'Du Ble "mal nécessaire". Réflexions sur les progrès de l'agriculture de 1750 à 1850', *Revue d'histoire moderne et contemporaine*, 26 (1979).

[85] Newell, W. H., 'The Agricultural Revolution in Nineteenth-Century France', *Journal of Economic History*, 33 (1973). The most direct challenge to the work of Morineau.

[86] Noiriel, G., *Longwy: immigrés et prolétaires, 1880–1980* (Paris, 1984).

[87] —, 'Du "Patronage" au "Paternalisme": la réstructuration des formes de domination de la main-d'oeuvre ouvrière dans l'industrie métallurgique française, *Le Mouvement social*, 144 (1988).

*[88] —, *Workers in French Society in the 19th and 20th Centuries* (New York, 1990). Provides a fruitful perspective for economic historians.

[89] Nye, J. V., 'Firm Size and Economic Backwardness: A New Look at the French Industrialization Debate', *Journal of Economic History*, 47 (1987).

[90] —, 'The Myth of Free-Trade Britain and Fortress France: Tariffs and Trade in the Nineteenth Century', *Journal of Economic History*, 51 (1991).

*[91] O'Brien, P. K. and Keyder, C., *Economic Growth in Britain and France, 1780–1914: Two Paths to the Twentieth Century* (London, 1978). The most extended and influential of the challenges to the 'retardation' school.

*[92] Perrot, M., 'The Three Ages of Industrial Discipline in Nineteenth-Century France', in J. M. Merriman (ed.), *Consciousness and Class Experience in Nineteenth-Century France* (New York, 1979).

[93] Price, R. 'The Onset of Labour Shortage in Nineteenth-Century French Agriculture', *Economic History Review*, 28 (1975).
*[94] —, *The Modernization of Rural France* (London, 1983). Particularly informative on the role of transport improvements.
[95] Reddy, W. M., *The Rise of Market Culture: The Textile Trade and French Society, 1750–1900* (Cambridge, 1984).
[96] Reid, D., *The Miners of Decazeville: A Genealogy of Deindustrialization* (Cambridge, Mass., 1985).
[97] R. Roehl, 'French Industrialization: A Reconsideration', *Explorations in Economic History*, 13 (1976). A truly 'seminal' article.
[98] —, 'Britain and European Industrialization: Pathfinder Pursued?', *Review* 6 (1983), 455–73.
[99] Ruttan, V. W., 'Structural Retardation and the Modernization of French Agriculture: A Skeptical View', *Journal of Economic History*, 38 (1978).
[100] Sawyer, J. E. 'The Entrepreneur and the Social Order', in W. Miller (ed.), *Men in Business* (Cambridge, Mass, 1952).
[101] Sewell, W., *Work and the Revolution in France: The Language of Labor from the Old Regime to 1848* (Cambridge, 1980).
[102] Thomson, J. K. J., *Clermont-de-Lodève, 1633–1789: Fluctuations in the Prosperity of a Languedocian Cloth-Making Town* (Cambridge, 1982). Argues an unfashionable thesis with great persuasiveness.
[103] Toutain, J.-C., 'The Uneven Growth of Regional Incomes in France from 1840 to 1970', in P. Bairoch and M. Lévy-Leboyer (eds), *Disparities in Economic Development since the Industrial Revolution* (London, 1981).
[104] Trebilcock, C., *The Industrialization of the Continental Powers, 1780–1914* (London, 1981). Includes a very full textbook account of French development, within an impressive analytical framework.
[105] Van Zanden, J. L., 'The First Green Revolution: The Growth of Production and Productivity in European Agriculture, 1870–1914', *Economic History Review*, 44 (1991).
[106] Woronoff, D., *L'Industrie sidérurgique en France pendant la Révolution et l'Empire* (Paris, 1984). Definitive study of the iron and steel industries between 1789 and 1815.

Index

New Studies in Economic and Social History

Titles in the series available from Cambridge University Press:

1. M. Anderson
   Approaches to the history of the Western family, 1500–1914
2. W. Macpherson
   The economic development of Japan, 1868–1941
3. R. Porter
   Disease, medicine, and society in England: second edition
4. B.W.E. Alford
   British economic performance since 1945
5. A. Crowther
   Social policy in Britain, 1914–1939
6. E. Roberts
   Women's work 1840–1940
7. C. O'Grada
   The great Irish famine
8. R. Rodger
   Housing in urban Britain 1780–1914
9. P. Slack
   The English Poor Law 1531–1782
10. J.L. Anderson
    Explaining long-term economic change
11. D. Baines
    Emigration from Europe 1815–1930

12. M. Collins
Banks and industrial finance 1800–1939

13. A. Dyer
Decline and growth in English towns 1400–1640

14. R.B. Outhwaite
Dearth, public policy and social disturbance in England, 1550–1800

15. M. Sanderson
Education, economic change and society in England

16. R.D. Anderson
Universities and elites in Britain since 1800

17. C. Heywood
The development of the French economy, 1700–1914

18. R.A. Houston
The population history of Britain and Ireland 1500–1750

19. A.J. Reid
Social classes and social relations in Britain 1850–1914

20. R. Woods
The population of Britain in the nineteenth century

21. T.C. Barker
The rise and rise of road transport, 1700–1990

22. J. Harrison
The Spanish economy

23. C. Schmitz
The growth of big business in the United States and Western Europe, 1850–1939

24. R.A. Church
The rise and decline of the British motor industry

25. P. Horn
Children's work and welfare, 1780–1880

26. R. Perren
Agriculture in depression, 1870–1940

27. R.J. Overy
The Nazi economic recovery 1932–1938: second edition

Previously published as

Studies in Economic History

Titles in the series available from the Macmillan Press Limited

1. B.W.E. Alford
   Depression and recovery? British economic growth, 1918–1939
2. M. Anderson
   Population change in north-western Europe, 1750–1850
3. S.D. Chapman
   The cotton industry in the industrial revolution: second edition
4. N. Charlesworth
   British rule and the Indian economy, 1800–1914
5. L.A. Clarkson
   Proto-industrialisation: the first phase of industrialisation
6. D.C. Coleman
   Industry in Tudor and Stuart England
7. I.M. Drummond
   The gold standard and the international monetary system, 1900–1939
8. M.E. Falkus
   The industrialisation of Russia, 1700–1914
9. J.R. Harris
   The British iron industry, 1700–1850
10. J. Hatcher
    Plague, population and the English economy, 1348–1530
11. J.R. Hay
    The origins of the Liberal welfare reforms, 1906–1914

12. H. McLeod
    Religion and the working classes in nineteenth-century Britain
13. J.D. Marshall
    The Old Poor Law 1795–1834: second edition
14. R.J. Morris
    Class and class consciousness in the industrial revolution, 1750–1850
15. P.K. O'Brien
    The economic effects of the American civil war
16. P.L. Payne
    British entrepreneurship in the nineteenth century
17. G.C. Peden
    Keynes, the treasury and British economic policy
18. M.E. Rose
    The relief of poverty, 1834–1914
19. J. Thirsk
    England's agricultural regions and agrarian history, 1500–1750
20. J.R. Ward
    Poverty and progress in the Caribbean, 1800–1960

Economic History Society

The Economic History Society, which numbers around 3,000 members, publishes the *Economic History Review* four times a year (free to members) and holds an annual conference.

Enquiries about membership should be addressed to

The Assistant Secretary
Economic History Society
PO Box 70
Kingswood
Bristol
BS15 5TB

Full-time students may join at special rates.